Kennedy's Great Mistake: Unveiling the Truth Behind the Watered-Down Bay of Pigs Invasion

Copyright Page

TITLE: Kennedy's Great Mistake: Unveiling the Truth Behind the Watered-Down Bay of Pigs Invasion

1ST Edition

ISBN: 9798223571841

Table of Contents

Kennedy's Great Mistake: Unveiling the Truth Behind the Watered-Down Bay of Pigs Invasion

By Roberto Miguel Rodriguez

Chapter 1: Kennedy's Great Mistake: Watering Down the Bay of Pigs Invasion for Fear of the Soviets

The Preparations for the Bay of Pigs Invasion

The Bay of Pigs Invasion, one of the most significant events of the Cold War era, was a pivotal moment in American history. This subchapter delves into the preparations made for this ill-fated operation, shedding light on the factors that led to its ultimate failure.

The planning for the Bay of Pigs Invasion began long before the actual event took place. In an attempt to overthrow Fidel Castro's communist regime in Cuba, President John F. Kennedy authorized the CIA to train and equip a group of Cuban exiles. These exiles were to serve as the main force to carry out the invasion.

However, as the invasion date drew near, it became clear that there were significant flaws in the operation. Kennedy, fearing Soviet retaliation and a potential escalation of the Cold War, made the controversial decision to water down the invasion plan. This decision would have far-reaching consequences, both politically and militarily.

From a political standpoint, Kennedy's decision had a profound impact on his reputation and the Democratic Party. The president's perceived weakness in the face of Soviet threats tarnished his image and undermined his credibility. The Democratic Party, already facing scrutiny for its handling of the Cold War, suffered a blow to its reputation as a strong defender against communism.

On a military level, the diluted invasion plan had disastrous consequences. The limited air support and inadequate resources provided to the Cuban exiles greatly hindered their chances of success.

The failure of the invasion highlighted the shortcomings of Kennedy's leadership style and decision-making process. Many historians have since analyzed how his approach influenced the outcome of the Bay of Pigs operation.

Another critical aspect to consider is the role of intelligence in the decision-making process. The subchapter investigates the intelligence failures and shortcomings that contributed to the decision to water down the invasion plan. By understanding these failures, historians can gain insight into the larger context surrounding the operation.

The media coverage and public perception of Kennedy's decision are also explored. The way the event was covered by the media and the public's reaction shed light on the political climate of the time. Additionally, the impact on the Cuban exile community, who were heavily involved in anti-Castro activities, is analyzed.

To provide a comprehensive understanding of the Bay of Pigs Invasion, the subchapter compares Kennedy's approach to previous administrations' policies toward Cuba and the Soviets. This contrast allows historians to appreciate the unique challenges and decisions faced by Kennedy during this critical period.

Furthermore, the international implications of Kennedy's decision are examined. The subchapter assesses how this decision affected US relations with other countries, particularly in Latin America and the Soviet Union.

Lastly, the subchapter delves into the long-term consequences of Kennedy's decision and its impact on future US foreign policy. By assessing the lessons learned from the Bay of Pigs Invasion, historians can gain valuable insights into the decision-making processes of future administrations.

In conclusion, the subchapter on the preparations for the Bay of Pigs Invasion provides historians with a comprehensive analysis of the factors that led to the diluted invasion plan. By addressing Kennedy's leadership style, intelligence failures, political fallout, military implications, and international implications, this subchapter offers a thorough examination of this pivotal moment in history. Moreover, by investigating conspiracy theories and alternative explanations, this subchapter invites historians to consider multiple perspectives and interpretations of the events surrounding the Bay of Pigs Invasion.

The Decision to Water Down the Invasion Plan

In the subchapter titled "The Decision to Water Down the Invasion Plan," the book "Kennedy's Great Mistake: Unveiling the Truth Behind the Watered-Down Bay of Pigs Invasion" delves into the circumstances and consequences of President John F. Kennedy's controversial decision to dilute the Bay of Pigs invasion plan. This chapter aims to provide historians with a comprehensive analysis of this critical moment in Cold War history, while also catering to the specific interests of niche audiences, such as those interested in Kennedy's leadership style, the political fallout of his decision, and the military implications.

The chapter begins by examining Kennedy's decision-making process and leadership style, shedding light on the factors that influenced his choice to water down the invasion plan. It explores his concerns about potential Soviet involvement and the repercussions this could have on US-Soviet relations during the tense Cold War era. By evaluating Kennedy's leadership style, the chapter aims to provide a deeper understanding of how his decision-making process influenced the outcome of the Bay of Pigs invasion.

The chapter also delves into the political fallout of Kennedy's decision, analyzing its impact on his reputation and the Democratic Party during the Cold War era. It explores the implications for US relations with other countries, particularly in Latin America and the Soviet Union, shedding light on the international consequences of Kennedy's decision.

Furthermore, the chapter investigates the military implications of the diluted invasion plan, assessing its impact on the military objectives and outcomes. It also delves into the role of intelligence, investigating the failures and shortcomings that contributed to the decision to water down the invasion plan.

The book also explores the public's perception of Kennedy's decision, analyzing media coverage and public opinion at the time. It discusses the role of the Cuban exile community and their subsequent involvement in anti-Castro activities, shedding light on the impact of Kennedy's decision on this community.

Additionally, the chapter compares Kennedy's approach to previous administrations' policies toward Cuba and the Soviets, highlighting the contrasts and similarities. It also delves into conspiracy theories and alternative explanations for Kennedy's decision, exploring their impact on historical interpretations.

Ultimately, the chapter aims to provide historians with a comprehensive analysis of the decision to water down the invasion plan, examining its political, military, and international implications. By doing so, it offers valuable insights into the long-term consequences of Kennedy's decision and its impact on future US foreign policy.

The Influence of Soviet Presence in Cuba

The presence of the Soviet Union in Cuba had a significant impact on the events leading up to and following the Bay of Pigs invasion. This subchapter delves into the various aspects of this influence, examining its political, military, and international implications. It also explores how the Soviet presence shaped Kennedy's decision-making process and leadership style, as well as the subsequent fallout and historical interpretations of his actions.

One of the key factors driving Kennedy's decision to water down the invasion plan was the fear of provoking a direct confrontation with the Soviets. The Cold War era was characterized by heightened tensions between the United States and the Soviet Union, and any move that could be perceived as an act of aggression risked escalating the conflict. Kennedy's desire to avoid a nuclear war influenced his approach to the Bay of Pigs invasion, ultimately leading to its failure.

The military implications of diluting the invasion plan were significant. By reducing the number of troops and airstrikes, Kennedy compromised the operation's chances of success. The strategic consequences of this decision were far-reaching, as it allowed the Cuban government to easily repel the invasion and reinforced Castro's grip on power. This failure had a lasting impact on the military objectives and outcomes of US interventions in Latin America.

Furthermore, the intelligence failures and shortcomings that contributed to the decision to water down the invasion plan cannot be overlooked. The CIA's flawed assessment of the situation in Cuba, coupled with inadequate intelligence gathering, played a crucial role in shaping Kennedy's perception of the risks involved. This subchapter investigates these intelligence failures and their impact on the overall decision-making process.

The Soviet presence in Cuba also had a profound impact on public opinion and media coverage of the Bay of Pigs invasion. The media's coverage of the event and the public's perception of Kennedy's decision were heavily influenced by Cold War sentiments and fears of communism. This subchapter explores how the media framed the invasion and its aftermath, as well as the public's reaction to Kennedy's handling of the situation.

Additionally, the Cuban exile community played a significant role in anti-Castro activities, both before and after the Bay of Pigs invasion. The subchapter analyzes how Kennedy's decision affected this community and their subsequent involvement in efforts to overthrow Castro's regime.

To fully understand the implications of Kennedy's approach to the Bay of Pigs invasion, it is essential to compare it to previous administrations' policies toward Cuba and the Soviets. This subchapter contrasts Kennedy's handling of the situation with the approaches taken by his predecessors, shedding light on the divergent strategies employed in dealing with the Cuban government and the Soviet Union.

Furthermore, the international implications of Kennedy's decision are examined, particularly in relation to US relations with other countries, especially those in Latin America and the Soviet Union. The subchapter explores how this incident affected US foreign policy and its standing in the international community.

Lastly, the subchapter delves into the long-term consequences of Kennedy's decision and its impact on future US foreign policy. It assesses the lessons learned from the Bay of Pigs invasion and how they shaped subsequent administrations' approaches to similar situations.

In conclusion, the influence of the Soviet presence in Cuba was a defining factor in Kennedy's decision to water down the Bay of Pigs invasion. This subchapter provides a comprehensive analysis of the political, military, and international implications of this influence, as well as its impact on Kennedy's leadership style, the intelligence failures surrounding the invasion, public opinion, the Cuban exile community, and historical interpretations of the event. By examining these aspects, historians can gain valuable insights into this critical moment in Cold War history and its lasting repercussions.

The Role of Fear and Cold War Politics

In the subchapter titled "The Role of Fear and Cold War Politics" in the book "Kennedy's Great Mistake: Unveiling the Truth Behind the Watered-Down Bay of Pigs Invasion," we delve into the complex web of fear and Cold War politics that influenced President Kennedy's decision to dilute the Bay of Pigs invasion plan. This chapter aims to provide historians with a comprehensive analysis of the various factors that contributed to this pivotal moment in American history.

Kennedy's Great Mistake explores how fear of the Soviets played a significant role in shaping Kennedy's decision-making process. The book examines the anxieties within the administration about provoking a military confrontation with the Soviet Union and the potential escalation of the Cold War. It delves into the prevailing mindset of containment and the fear of Soviet retaliation, which ultimately led to the watering down of the invasion plan.

The political fallout of Kennedy's decision is another crucial aspect examined in this chapter. By analyzing the impact on Kennedy's reputation and the Democratic Party during the Cold War era, historians can gain insights into the long-term consequences of this decision. The book scrutinizes how the Bay of Pigs invasion became a defining moment in Kennedy's presidency and affected public perception of his leadership abilities.

Furthermore, the military implications of the diluted invasion plan are explored in-depth. By examining the strategic consequences and the impact on military objectives and outcomes, historians can gain a comprehensive understanding of the repercussions of Kennedy's decision. The book evaluates how the diluted plan undermined the chances of success and contributed to the failure of the invasion.

The chapter also delves into Kennedy's leadership style, investigating how it influenced the Bay of Pigs invasion. By analyzing Kennedy's decision-making process, historians can gain insights into his approach to crisis management and his ability to navigate the complexities of Cold War politics.

The role of intelligence failures and shortcomings is another crucial aspect investigated in this chapter. By investigating the intelligence failures that contributed to the decision to water down the invasion plan, historians can gain insights into the limitations of the U.S. intelligence apparatus during this period.

Additionally, the chapter explores the media coverage and public perception of Kennedy's decision. By exploring how the media covered the event and the public's perception, historians can gain insights into the broader societal impact of the Bay of Pigs invasion.

The impact on the Cuban exile community is also analyzed, examining how Kennedy's decision affected this community and their subsequent role in anti-Castro activities.

Furthermore, by contrasting Kennedy's handling of the Bay of Pigs invasion with previous administrations' policies toward Cuba and the Soviets, historians can gain insights into the continuity and change in American foreign policy.

The international implications of Kennedy's decision are also examined, particularly in relation to U.S. relations with other countries, especially in Latin America and the Soviet Union.

The chapter concludes by assessing the long-term consequences of Kennedy's decision and its impact on future U.S. foreign policy. By evaluating the lessons learned from the Bay of Pigs invasion, historians can gain insights into the formulation of subsequent foreign policy decisions.

Finally, the chapter investigates conspiracy theories and alternative interpretations of Kennedy's decision. By exploring these theories and their impact on historical interpretations, historians can gain a broader perspective on the motivations and influences behind the decision to dilute the invasion plan.

The Immediate Consequences of the Diluted Invasion Plan

The Bay of Pigs invasion, a pivotal event in the history of the Cold War, was meant to be a decisive blow against the communist regime of Fidel Castro in Cuba. However, President John F. Kennedy's decision to water down the invasion plan had immediate consequences that reverberated across various aspects of American society and foreign policy.

One of the most significant repercussions was the political fallout for Kennedy himself and the Democratic Party. Kennedy's reputation took a severe hit as critics accused him of weakness and indecisiveness in the face of Soviet aggression. This event marked a turning point in his presidency, eroding his image as a strong leader in the fight against communism. Moreover, the Democratic Party faced a crisis of confidence, as many questioned its ability to effectively combat the spread of communism.

The military implications of the diluted invasion plan were also profound. By reducing the scale and intensity of the operation, the chances of success were significantly diminished. The lack of air support and limited resources hampered the military objectives, leading to a resounding defeat for the Cuban exiles. This failure not only tarnished the reputation of the United States military but also highlighted the Soviet Union's growing influence in the region.

Kennedy's decision-making process and leadership style came under scrutiny in the aftermath of the Bay of Pigs invasion. Many historians have analyzed how his fear of provoking a direct confrontation with the Soviets influenced his choice to water down the invasion plan. This event revealed a caution and hesitancy in Kennedy's leadership style, contrasting sharply with his rhetoric of boldness and determination.

The role of intelligence failures and shortcomings cannot be overstated in understanding the decision to dilute the invasion plan. The CIA's flawed assessments and overconfidence in the support of the Cuban population played a significant role in underestimating the resistance the exiles would face. This failure in intelligence gathering and analysis further exacerbated the consequences of the diluted invasion plan.

Public opinion and media coverage also played a crucial role in shaping the immediate aftermath of the Bay of Pigs invasion. The media covered the event extensively, exposing the failures and inadequacies of the operation. This negative coverage not only damaged Kennedy's reputation but also influenced public perception of his decision-making abilities.

The Cuban exile community, which had pinned its hopes on the success of the invasion, was left disillusioned and marginalized. Many exiles felt betrayed by Kennedy's decision to scale back the operation, leading to a shift in their political activism and subsequent involvement in anti-Castro activities.

Internationally, Kennedy's decision had far-reaching implications. It strained US relations with Latin American countries, as they viewed the failure of the invasion as a sign of American weakness.

Furthermore, it emboldened the Soviet Union, which saw the United States as vulnerable and indecisive.

The immediate consequences of the diluted invasion plan were profound and far-reaching. They impacted Kennedy's reputation and the Democratic Party, exposed weaknesses in American military capabilities, and influenced public opinion and international relations. Understanding these consequences is essential in comprehending the full extent of Kennedy's great mistake and its impact on future US foreign policy.

Chapter 2: The Political Fallout of Kennedy's Decision: Analyzing the Impact on Kennedy's Reputation and the Democratic Party during the Cold War Era

Kennedy's Reputation Before the Bay of Pigs

Before the infamous Bay of Pigs invasion, President John F. Kennedy had established himself as a promising leader, full of charisma and charm. Kennedy's great mistake, however, tarnished his reputation and had far-reaching consequences. This subchapter delves into Kennedy's reputation before the Bay of Pigs invasion, exploring how his leadership style and decision-making process ultimately led to a watered-down plan that failed to achieve its objectives.

Kennedy's Great Mistake: Watering Down the Bay of Pigs Invasion for Fear of the Soviets

One of the key reasons behind Kennedy's decision to dilute the invasion plan was his fear of Soviet retaliation. As historians, it is crucial to analyze how Kennedy's concerns about the Soviets and their potential involvement in the conflict influenced his decision-making process. By examining Kennedy's leadership style, we can gain a deeper understanding of why he opted for a more cautious approach, even though it ultimately compromised the mission's chances of success.

The Political Fallout of Kennedy's Decision: Analyzing the Impact on Kennedy's Reputation and the Democratic Party during the Cold War Era

Kennedy's reputation took a significant hit following the failure of the Bay of Pigs invasion. This subchapter delves into the political fallout, exploring how the invasion's failure impacted Kennedy's standing within the Democratic Party and the broader political landscape during the Cold War era. By evaluating the long-term consequences of this decision, historians can gain insights into the challenges faced by Kennedy and his administration in the aftermath of the failed invasion.

The Military Implications: Examining the Strategic Consequences of the Diluted Invasion Plan on the Military Objectives and Outcomes

By examining the diluted invasion plan, historians can evaluate the military implications of Kennedy's decision. This subchapter delves into the strategic consequences of the watered-down plan, analyzing how it affected the military objectives and outcomes of the mission. By understanding the impact of Kennedy's decision on the ground, we can gain insights into the challenges faced by the military during the Bay of Pigs invasion.

Evaluating Kennedy's Leadership Style: Delving into Kennedy's Decision-Making Process and Leadership Style, and Analyzing How It Influenced the Bay of Pigs Invasion

Kennedy's leadership style played a crucial role in the decision to water down the invasion plan. By examining his decision-making process and leadership style, historians can gain insights into how Kennedy's approach influenced the outcome of the Bay of Pigs invasion. This subchapter delves into the factors that shaped Kennedy's decision-making and explores how his leadership style influenced the course of events.

The Role of Intelligence: Investigating the Intelligence Failures and Shortcomings That Contributed to the Decision to Water Down the Invasion Plan

Intelligence failures and shortcomings were instrumental in shaping Kennedy's decision to dilute the invasion plan. This subchapter investigates the role of intelligence in the decision-making process, analyzing the failures and shortcomings that contributed to the misjudgment. By understanding the intelligence landscape at the time, historians can gain a comprehensive view of the factors that influenced Kennedy's decision.

Public Opinion and Media Coverage: Exploring How the Media Covered the Event and the Public's Perception of Kennedy's Decision

The Bay of Pigs invasion garnered significant media attention and had a profound impact on public opinion. This subchapter explores how the media covered the event and delves into the public's perception of Kennedy's decision to water down the invasion plan. By examining the media's role and the public's reaction, historians can gain insights into the broader societal implications of the Bay of Pigs invasion.

The Cuban Exile Community: Analyzing the Impact on the Cuban Exile Community and Their Subsequent Role in Anti-Castro Activities

The Cuban exile community played a crucial role in the Bay of Pigs invasion and its aftermath. By analyzing the impact of Kennedy's decision on the Cuban exile community, historians can gain insights into their subsequent activities and resistance against the Castro regime. This subchapter delves into the experiences and actions of the Cuban exiles, shedding light on their role in anti-Castro activities.

Comparing Kennedy's Approach to Previous Administrations: Contrasting Kennedy's Handling of the Bay of Pigs Invasion with Previous Administrations' Policies Toward Cuba and the Soviets

To fully understand Kennedy's approach to the Bay of Pigs invasion, it is crucial to compare it with the policies of previous administrations. This subchapter contrasts Kennedy's handling of the invasion with the approaches of previous administrations toward Cuba and the Soviets.

By examining the continuity or divergence in policies, historians can gain a comprehensive understanding of the factors that influenced Kennedy's decision.

International Implications: Examining How Kennedy's Decision Affected US Relations with Other Countries, Particularly in Latin America and the Soviet Union

Kennedy's decision to water down the invasion plan had significant international implications. This subchapter examines how Kennedy's decision affected U.S. relations with other countries, particularly in Latin America and the Soviet Union. By analyzing the diplomatic fallout and the responses of other nations, historians can gain insights into the broader international context of the Bay of Pigs invasion.

Lessons Learned: Assessing the Long-Term Consequences of Kennedy's Decision and Its Impact on Future US Foreign Policy

The Bay of Pigs invasion had long-term consequences for U.S. foreign policy. This subchapter assesses the lessons learned from Kennedy's decision and analyzes its impact on future foreign policy decisions. By evaluating the consequences of the invasion, historians can gain insights into the factors that shaped U.S. foreign policy in the years to come.

Conspiracy Theories and Alternate Interpretations: Investigating Conspiracy Theories and Alternative Explanations for Kennedy's Decision to Water Down the Invasion Plan, and Their Impact on Historical Interpretations

Throughout history, conspiracy theories and alternative explanations have emerged to challenge official narratives. This subchapter investigates conspiracy theories and alternative interpretations surrounding Kennedy's decision to water down the invasion plan. By critically examining these theories, historians can gain a nuanced understanding of the various perspectives and their impact on historical interpretations.

The Effect on Kennedy's Political Career

The Bay of Pigs invasion is widely regarded as one of the most significant events in John F. Kennedy's presidency. Its impact on Kennedy's political career cannot be overstated, as it shaped public perception of his leadership abilities and had far-reaching consequences for both the Democratic Party and US foreign policy during the Cold War era.

Kennedy's decision to water down the Bay of Pigs invasion plan for fear of the Soviets had a profound effect on his reputation. Historians have analyzed the political fallout of this decision, highlighting its implications for Kennedy's standing among both domestic and international audiences. This subchapter delves into the various factors that contributed to the negative perception of Kennedy's leadership, including his decision-making process and leadership style.

One aspect that is examined is the role of intelligence in the decision-making process. Investigating the intelligence failures and shortcomings that led to the decision to dilute the invasion plan sheds light on the factors that influenced Kennedy's choices. Furthermore, the subchapter explores the media coverage of the event and the public's perception of Kennedy's decision, providing insight into how it affected his political career.

The impact on the Cuban exile community is also explored, as the invasion had a profound effect on their lives and subsequent involvement in anti-Castro activities. Additionally, the subchapter compares Kennedy's approach to previous administrations' policies toward Cuba and the Soviets, highlighting the differences and similarities in their handling of the situation.

Internationally, Kennedy's decision affected US relations with other countries, particularly in Latin America and with the Soviet Union. The subchapter analyzes these international implications, providing a comprehensive understanding of the broader consequences of Kennedy's actions.

Furthermore, the subchapter assesses the long-term consequences of Kennedy's decision and its impact on future US foreign policy. It explores the lessons learned from the Bay of Pigs invasion and how they influenced subsequent administrations' approaches to similar situations.

Lastly, the subchapter delves into conspiracy theories and alternative explanations for Kennedy's decision to water down the invasion plan. By investigating these theories and their impact on historical interpretations, the subchapter provides a comprehensive overview of the various perspectives on this critical event in Kennedy's political career.

In conclusion, the Bay of Pigs invasion had a profound effect on John F. Kennedy's political career. This subchapter examines the impact on Kennedy's reputation, the Democratic Party, and US foreign policy, as well as the various factors that influenced his decision-making process. By addressing the perspectives of historians and the niches interested in this topic, it offers a comprehensive analysis of the effect of the Bay of Pigs invasion on Kennedy's political career.

The Democratic Party's Response to the Bay of Pigs

"The Democratic Party's Response to the Bay of Pigs"

The Bay of Pigs invasion is a pivotal event in American history, particularly in the context of the Cold War era. In this subchapter, we will delve into the Democratic Party's response to this ill-fated mission and its broader implications for President John F. Kennedy, the party, and the United States as a whole.

Kennedy's Great Mistake: Watering Down the Bay of Pigs Invasion for Fear of the Soviets

One of the key aspects we will explore is the decision-making process behind the watering down of the invasion plan. We will analyze Kennedy's leadership style and how it influenced this crucial event. By examining the political fallout of his decision, we can assess the impact on his reputation and the Democratic Party's standing during this critical period of the Cold War.

The Political Fallout of Kennedy's Decision: Analyzing the Impact on Kennedy's Reputation and the Democratic Party during the Cold War Era

We will also examine the role of intelligence failures and shortcomings that contributed to the decision to water down the invasion plan. By investigating how the media covered the event and the public's perception of Kennedy's decision, we can gain insight into the impact on the Cuban exile community and their subsequent role in anti-Castro activities.

The Military Implications: Examining the Strategic Consequences of the Diluted Invasion Plan on the Military Objectives and Outcomes

Furthermore, we will assess the strategic consequences of the diluted invasion plan on the military objectives and outcomes. By comparing Kennedy's approach to previous administrations' policies toward Cuba and the Soviets, we can shed light on the broader implications of his decision.

International Implications: Examining How Kennedy's Decision Affected US Relations with Other Countries, Particularly in Latin America and the Soviet Union

Additionally, we will explore how Kennedy's decision affected US relations with other countries, particularly in Latin America and the Soviet Union. By assessing the long-term consequences of Kennedy's decision, we can better understand its impact on future US foreign policy.

Lessons Learned: Assessing the Long-Term Consequences of Kennedy's Decision and Its Impact on Future US Foreign Policy

Finally, we will delve into conspiracy theories and alternative explanations for Kennedy's decision to water down the invasion plan. By investigating these theories and their impact on historical interpretations, we can gain a more comprehensive understanding of this critical moment in American history.

In conclusion, this subchapter will provide historians, as well as those interested in Kennedy's Great Mistake, with a comprehensive analysis of the Democratic Party's response to the Bay of Pigs invasion. By exploring the political, military, intelligence, and international implications of Kennedy's decision, we can gain valuable insights into US foreign policy during the Cold War era and its long-term consequences.

Public Perception and Approval Ratings

The Bay of Pigs invasion was a pivotal moment in American history, and it had significant implications for both domestic and international affairs. One crucial aspect that cannot be overlooked is the public perception and approval ratings surrounding President John F. Kennedy's decision to water down the invasion plan. This subchapter delves into the various factors that influenced public opinion and media coverage during this critical period.

From the outset, Kennedy's Great Mistake: Watering Down the Bay of Pig Invasion for Fear of the Soviets examines the political fallout of Kennedy's decision and its impact on his reputation and the Democratic Party during the Cold War era. Historians have long debated the motivations behind Kennedy's choice to scale back the operation. Some argue that his primary concern was preventing direct confrontation with the Soviet Union, fearing an escalation into a larger conflict. Others believe that Kennedy's decision was driven by a desire to distance himself from the aggressive policies of previous administrations.

The media played a significant role in shaping public opinion on the Bay of Pigs invasion. Journalists portrayed the operation as a failure, highlighting the lack of support from the local population and the Cuban exile community. The American public was bombarded with images of defeated and captured Cuban exiles, further eroding support for the invasion. This subchapter explores the media's coverage of the event and how it influenced the public's perception of Kennedy's decision.

Furthermore, the subchapter examines the impact on the Cuban exile community and their subsequent role in anti-Castro activities. Many exiles felt betrayed by Kennedy's decision to dilute the invasion plan, leading them to question his commitment to their cause. The subchapter delves into the long-term consequences of this disillusionment and its impact on the Cuban exile community's involvement in anti-Castro efforts.

Additionally, this subchapter compares Kennedy's approach to previous administrations' policies toward Cuba and the Soviets. By contrasting Kennedy's handling of the Bay of Pigs invasion with previous administrations' more aggressive tactics, historians can gain insight into the unique challenges Kennedy faced and the factors that influenced his decision-making process.

Finally, the subchapter explores the international implications of Kennedy's decision. It examines how this event affected US relations with other countries, particularly in Latin America and the Soviet Union. By evaluating these international repercussions, historians can better understand the broader significance of Kennedy's decision and its impact on future US foreign policy.

In conclusion, this subchapter on public perception and approval ratings provides a comprehensive analysis of the factors that shaped public opinion and media coverage surrounding Kennedy's decision to water down the Bay of Pigs invasion. By examining the political fallout, media coverage, impact on the Cuban exile community, and international implications, historians can gain a more nuanced understanding of this critical moment in American history and its lasting consequences.

The Long-Term Political Consequences

In the annals of American history, few events have had such far-reaching political consequences as President John F. Kennedy's decision to water down the Bay of Pigs invasion. This subchapter delves into the long-term political fallout of this ill-fated decision during the Cold War era. Addressed to historians, it aims to shed light on the impact of Kennedy's choice on his reputation, the Democratic Party, and the broader geopolitical landscape.

Kennedy's Great Mistake: Watering Down the Bay of Pigs Invasion for Fear of the Soviets

The political fallout of Kennedy's decision was immense. By choosing to reduce the scale of the invasion plan for fear of provoking the

Soviets, Kennedy inadvertently sent a message of weakness to both his domestic and international audiences. Critics argued that this move undermined American credibility and emboldened the Soviet Union, ultimately eroding trust in the Kennedy administration's ability to confront Communist threats.

Analyzing the Impact on Kennedy's Reputation and the Democratic Party during the Cold War Era

Kennedy's leadership style and decision-making process played a pivotal role in the Bay of Pigs debacle. This subchapter delves into these aspects, examining how Kennedy's approach affected the invasion's strategic objectives and outcomes. Furthermore, it explores the subsequent damage to Kennedy's reputation and the Democratic Party's standing during a crucial period of the Cold War.

The Role of Intelligence and Media Coverage

Investigating the intelligence failures and shortcomings that contributed to the decision to water down the invasion plan, this subchapter sheds light on the critical role of accurate information in shaping foreign policy decisions. It also explores how the media covered the event and the subsequent impact on public perception of Kennedy's leadership.

International Implications and Lessons Learned

The consequences of Kennedy's decision extended beyond domestic politics. This subchapter examines how Kennedy's choice affected US relations with other countries, particularly in Latin America and the Soviet Union. It emphasizes the importance of understanding these international implications for comprehending the broader context of the Cold War.

Conspiracy Theories and Alternate Interpretations

As with any significant historical event, conspiracy theories and alternative explanations have emerged surrounding Kennedy's decision. This subchapter investigates these theories and their impact on historical interpretations, highlighting the need for critical analysis and considering multiple perspectives.

In conclusion, the long-term political consequences of Kennedy's decision to water down the Bay of Pigs invasion were profound. From damaging Kennedy's reputation and the Democratic Party to influencing US relations with other nations, this subchapter provides a comprehensive analysis of the far-reaching effects of this pivotal event in American history.

Chapter 3: The Military Implications: Examining the Strategic Consequences of the Diluted Invasion Plan on the Military Objectives and Outcomes

The Original Military Objectives

In this subchapter, we delve into the original military objectives of the Bay of Pigs invasion and how they were impacted by President Kennedy's decision to water down the plan. Historians and those interested in Kennedy's Great Mistake: Watering Down the Bay of Pigs Invasion for Fear of the Soviets will find this section particularly enlightening.

The Bay of Pigs invasion was initially conceived as a bold and decisive military operation aimed at overthrowing Fidel Castro's communist regime in Cuba. The original plan, developed under the Eisenhower administration, involved a full-scale invasion by a force of Cuban exiles trained and equipped by the United States. The objectives were clear: to eliminate the Castro regime, establish a democratic government, and roll back the spread of communism in the Western Hemisphere.

However, as we explore in this subchapter, President Kennedy, fearful of provoking a direct confrontation with the Soviet Union, decided to water down the invasion plan. Instead of providing air cover and adequate support for the exiled forces, Kennedy decided to limit U.S. involvement, leading to disastrous consequences.

By analyzing the military implications of this decision, we examine how the diluted invasion plan undermined the original objectives. The lack of air cover allowed Castro's forces to easily repel the exiled forces, leading to their capture and imprisonment. The failure of the invasion not only strengthened Castro's regime but also damaged Kennedy's reputation and the Democratic Party during the Cold War era, a topic of interest for historians exploring the political fallout of Kennedy's decision.

Furthermore, we evaluate Kennedy's leadership style and decision-making process, analyzing how it influenced the Bay of Pigs invasion. His cautious approach and reliance on limited intelligence contributed to the intelligence failures and shortcomings that ultimately led to the decision to water down the invasion plan. The role of intelligence in shaping the outcome of the invasion and its impact on historical interpretations are also explored in this subchapter.

Additionally, we examine the impact of Kennedy's decision on the Cuban exile community and their subsequent role in anti-Castro activities. We also compare Kennedy's approach to previous administrations' policies toward Cuba and the Soviets, highlighting the contrasts and implications for U.S. foreign policy.

Finally, we explore the international implications of Kennedy's decision, particularly its effect on U.S. relations with other countries, such as Latin American nations and the Soviet Union. We assess the long-term consequences of Kennedy's decision and its impact on future U.S. foreign policy, drawing lessons from this pivotal event in history.

Throughout this subchapter, we also investigate conspiracy theories and alternative explanations for Kennedy's decision, providing a comprehensive analysis of the Bay of Pigs invasion and its far-reaching effects. This section will surely enlighten historians and those interested in understanding the truth behind Kennedy's Great Mistake.

The Impact of the Watered-Down Invasion Plan on Success

"The Impact of the Watered-Down Invasion Plan on Success"

Introduction:

The Bay of Pigs invasion of 1961 remains one of the most controversial episodes in American history. President John F. Kennedy's decision to water down the invasion plan had far-reaching consequences, affecting not only the military objectives and outcomes but also the political fallout, Kennedy's reputation, and US foreign policy. This subchapter aims to delve into the multifaceted impact of the diluted invasion plan on the success of the operation, exploring various perspectives and shedding light on the historical significance of Kennedy's great mistake.

I. The Political Fallout:

Kennedy's decision to weaken the invasion plan had severe repercussions on his reputation and the Democratic Party during the height of the Cold War. Historians will analyze how this controversial move affected Kennedy's standing among his allies, the public's perception of his leadership, and the subsequent political climate in the United States.

II. Military Implications:

Examining the strategic consequences of the watered-down invasion plan is crucial to understanding the operation's failure. Historians will delve into the military objectives and outcomes, assessing the impact of the weakened plan on the invasion's success, or lack thereof. They will analyze the tactical errors, logistical challenges, and the overall effectiveness of the operation.

III. Evaluating Kennedy's Leadership Style:

Kennedy's decision-making process and leadership style will be scrutinized to shed light on how they influenced the Bay of Pigs invasion. Historians will explore the political and personal factors that shaped Kennedy's choices, offering insights into his decision to dilute the invasion plan and the ramifications of such a move.

IV. The Role of Intelligence:

Investigating the intelligence failures and shortcomings that contributed to the decision to water down the invasion plan is crucial in understanding the events leading up to the Bay of Pigs. Historians will analyze the available intelligence at the time, the assessments made by intelligence agencies, and the implications of their inaccuracies on the decision-making process.

V. Public Opinion and Media Coverage:

Exploring the media's coverage of the Bay of Pigs invasion and the public's perception of Kennedy's decision is essential to understanding the aftermath of the operation. Historians will examine how the media framed the event, the public's reaction to the invasion's failure, and the long-term impact on Kennedy's presidency.

VI. The Cuban Exile Community:

Analyzing the impact of the diluted invasion plan on the Cuban exile community is crucial to understanding their subsequent role in anti-Castro activities. Historians will explore how their disappointment and frustration with Kennedy's decision shaped their actions and contributed to the broader anti-Castro movement.

VII. Lessons Learned:

Assessing the long-term consequences of Kennedy's decision is paramount in understanding its impact on future US foreign policy. Historians will explore how this event influenced subsequent administrations' approach to Cuba and other geopolitical challenges, offering valuable insights into the lessons learned from Kennedy's great mistake.

VIII. Conspiracy Theories and Alternate Interpretations:

Investigating conspiracy theories and alternative explanations for Kennedy's decision to water down the invasion plan is essential to understanding the diverse interpretations of this historical event. Historians will critically analyze these theories and their impact on shaping historical narratives surrounding the Bay of Pigs invasion.

Conclusion:

The impact of the watered-down invasion plan on the success of the Bay of Pigs operation was far-reaching, affecting not only military outcomes but also political, social, and international dynamics. By delving into these different dimensions, historians can provide a comprehensive understanding of Kennedy's great mistake and its lasting implications on US history and foreign policy.

The Failure to Secure Air Superiority

In the subchapter titled "The Failure to Secure Air Superiority," we delve into one of the critical aspects that contributed to the lackluster outcome of the Bay of Pigs invasion. Addressing a niche audience of historians, this section of the book "Kennedy's Great Mistake: Unveiling the Truth Behind the Watered-Down Bay of Pigs Invasion" explores the military implications of the diluted invasion plan on the strategic objectives and outcomes.

The Bay of Pigs invasion was initially conceived as a bold and audacious plan to overthrow Fidel Castro's regime in Cuba. However, the decision to water down the invasion plan due to fears of Soviet intervention had significant consequences, particularly in securing air superiority.

One of the key elements of the original plan was the crucial role of air support. It was believed that air superiority would be the linchpin for the success of the invasion. The plan called for airstrikes to neutralize the Cuban air force, thereby paving the way for the amphibious assault by the Cuban exiles. However, the decision to limit airstrikes to avoid provoking the Soviets rendered the invasion vulnerable and severely compromised its chances of success.

This subchapter examines the strategic consequences of the failure to secure air superiority. The absence of a decisive air campaign allowed Castro's forces to maintain control of the skies, leading to devastating consequences for the invading forces. Without adequate air cover, the exiled fighters faced heavy resistance and were quickly overwhelmed, resulting in a catastrophic defeat.

Furthermore, this section also evaluates Kennedy's leadership style and decision-making process, analyzing how it influenced the dilution of the invasion plan. By succumbing to the fear of provoking the Soviets, Kennedy made a crucial error in judgment, which had far-reaching implications not only for the military objectives but also for his reputation and the Democratic Party during the Cold War era.

In addition, the role of intelligence failures and shortcomings that contributed to the decision to water down the invasion plan is investigated. This subchapter also explores the media coverage and public opinion surrounding Kennedy's decision, shedding light on the public's perception of the event.

By dissecting the failure to secure air superiority, this subchapter offers historians a deeper understanding of the Bay of Pigs invasion and its consequences. It provides valuable insights into the military implications, leadership style, intelligence failures, and public perception, shedding light on the complexities of this pivotal moment in history.

The Role of Cuban Military and Defense

The Cuban military and defense played a significant role in the events surrounding the Bay of Pigs invasion, highlighting the complexities and challenges faced by both the invading forces and the Cuban government. This subchapter will delve into the various aspects of the Cuban military's involvement, shedding light on their strategies, capabilities, and the ultimate outcome of the invasion.

The Cuban military, under the leadership of Fidel Castro, proved to be a formidable force during the Bay of Pigs invasion. With a well-trained army and extensive support from the Soviet Union, the Cuban military was well-prepared to defend their homeland. They swiftly mobilized their troops and effectively utilized their resources to repel the invading forces.

One of the key factors that contributed to the success of the Cuban military was their knowledge of the local terrain and the support they received from the Cuban population. This intimate familiarity with their surroundings allowed them to launch effective counterattacks, ambushing the invading forces and thwarting their advances.

Furthermore, the Cuban military's close alliance with the Soviet Union played a crucial role in their defense. The Soviets provided Cuba with advanced weaponry, including surface-to-air missiles, which proved to be instrumental in repelling airstrikes from the invading forces. This military support from the Soviets showcased the international implications of the invasion, as it highlighted the Soviet Union's commitment to defending their allies and challenging U.S. influence in the region.

Additionally, the Cuban military's success in repelling the invasion had significant political ramifications. The victory bolstered Castro's regime, solidifying his position as a leader who could defend Cuba against external threats. It also served as a rallying point for the Cuban population, bolstering their support for the revolution and the socialist government.

In conclusion, the role of the Cuban military and defense in the Bay of Pigs invasion cannot be understated. Their strategic prowess, support from the Soviet Union, and familiarity with the local terrain played a crucial role in repelling the invading forces. The Cuban military's success not only had immediate political implications but also had long-term consequences, as it solidified Castro's regime and further strained U.S.-Cuba relations. Understanding the role of the Cuban military in this event provides valuable insights into the complexities of the Cold War era and the challenges faced by both sides in this conflict.

Lessons Learned for Future Military Operations

In the aftermath of the Bay of Pigs invasion, there are several key lessons that can be learned for future military operations. This chapter will delve into these lessons and their implications for the Kennedy administration, the United States, and future foreign policy decisions.

Firstly, it is crucial to evaluate Kennedy's leadership style and decision-making process. The Bay of Pigs invasion was plagued by a lack of coordination and clear objectives, which can be attributed to Kennedy's hands-off approach and reliance on his advisors. This highlights the importance of strong leadership and clear communication in military operations.

Additionally, the role of intelligence cannot be underestimated. The intelligence failures and shortcomings that contributed to the decision to water down the invasion plan must be thoroughly investigated. This includes analyzing the sources of information, the accuracy of the intelligence, and the impact it had on the decision-making process.

Future military operations must prioritize accurate and reliable intelligence to avoid similar pitfalls.

The political fallout of Kennedy's decision also warrants examination. The impact on Kennedy's reputation and the Democratic Party during the Cold War era cannot be ignored. The media coverage and public opinion of the event played a significant role in shaping the narrative surrounding the invasion. Understanding how the media covered the event and the public's perception of Kennedy's decision can provide valuable insights for future leaders.

Furthermore, the strategic consequences of the diluted invasion plan on military objectives and outcomes must be evaluated. This includes analyzing the impact on the Cuban exile community and their subsequent role in anti-Castro activities. The long-term consequences of Kennedy's decision and its impact on future US foreign policy should also be assessed.

Comparing Kennedy's approach to previous administrations' policies toward Cuba and the Soviets is essential. By contrasting Kennedy's handling of the Bay of Pigs invasion with previous administrations, valuable lessons can be learned for future leaders in terms of foreign policy and national security.

Lastly, it is important to address conspiracy theories and alternative interpretations of Kennedy's decision. Investigating these theories and their impact on historical interpretations can provide a more nuanced understanding of the events surrounding the Bay of Pigs invasion.

Overall, the lessons learned from the Bay of Pigs invasion should serve as a cautionary tale for future military operations. By thoroughly analyzing the political, military, and intelligence aspects of the invasion, historians can glean valuable insights to inform future decision-making processes and prevent similar mistakes from occurring.

Chapter 4: Evaluating Kennedy's Leadership Style: Delving into Kennedy's Decision-Making Process and Leadership Style, and Analyzing How It Influenced the Bay of Pigs Invasion

Kennedy's Leadership Approach

In the subchapter titled "Kennedy's Leadership Approach," we delve into President John F. Kennedy's decision-making process and leadership style, analyzing how it influenced the Bay of Pigs invasion. This section is aimed at historians and focuses on understanding the intricacies of Kennedy's approach to the crisis.

Kennedy, known for his charismatic and eloquent style, faced a critical juncture during the Cold War era when the Bay of Pigs invasion was being planned. The invasion aimed to overthrow Fidel Castro's regime in Cuba, which was seen as a growing threat to American interests in the region. However, Kennedy's leadership approach took an unexpected turn, as he chose to water down the invasion plan out of fear of Soviet retaliation.

By examining Kennedy's decision-making process, we aim to shed light on the factors that influenced his approach. We analyze the impact on Kennedy's reputation and the Democratic Party during this critical moment, considering the political fallout of his decision. Additionally, we explore the strategic consequences of the diluted invasion plan on the military objectives and outcomes, assessing the implications for the United States.

Furthermore, this subchapter investigates the role of intelligence in shaping Kennedy's approach. We examine the intelligence failures and shortcomings that contributed to the decision to dilute the invasion plan, shedding light on the complexities of gathering accurate information during this period of heightened tensions.

Public opinion and media coverage also played a crucial role in shaping the aftermath of the Bay of Pigs invasion. We explore how the media covered the event and the public's perception of Kennedy's decision, analyzing its impact on his leadership and public support.

Moreover, we assess the impact on the Cuban exile community, who had been hoping for a stronger and more successful invasion. We delve into the consequences for the Cuban exile community and their subsequent role in anti-Castro activities, exploring their response to Kennedy's leadership approach.

Comparing Kennedy's approach to previous administrations' policies toward Cuba and the Soviets provides a comprehensive understanding of the decision-making process. By contrasting Kennedy's handling of the Bay of Pigs invasion with previous administrations, we gain insights into the unique challenges that Kennedy faced and how his leadership style differed from his predecessors.

Furthermore, this subchapter examines the international implications of Kennedy's decision. We analyze how it affected US relations with other countries, particularly in Latin America and the Soviet Union, taking into account the broader global context of the Cold War era.

Lastly, we consider the long-term consequences of Kennedy's decision and its impact on future US foreign policy. By assessing the lessons learned from this pivotal moment in history, we gain a deeper understanding of how it shaped subsequent approaches to foreign affairs.

Additionally, we investigate conspiracy theories and alternative explanations for Kennedy's decision to water down the invasion plan. By exploring these alternate interpretations, we shed light on the complexities of historical analysis and the impact of different perspectives on our understanding of this crucial event.

In conclusion, the subchapter "Kennedy's Leadership Approach" provides historians with a comprehensive analysis of Kennedy's decision-making process, leadership style, and the various factors that influenced the Bay of Pigs invasion. By examining the political, military, intelligence, and public opinion aspects, we gain a deeper understanding of this critical moment in history and its long-term consequences.

The Decision-Making Process Leading to the Diluted Plan

In this subchapter, we delve into the decision-making process that ultimately led to the watering down of the Bay of Pigs invasion plan. Addressing the audience of historians and the niches interested in Kennedy's Great Mistake, we aim to unveil the truth behind this critical event in Cold War history.

Kennedy's Great Mistake: Watering Down the Bay of Pig Invasion for Fear of the Soviets

One of the primary factors that led to the diluted plan was Kennedy's fear of provoking the Soviet Union. As tensions escalated during the Cold War, the President was concerned about the potential nuclear retaliation from the Soviets if the invasion went ahead as originally planned. This fear of a direct confrontation with the Soviet Union heavily influenced the decision-making process.

The Political Fallout of Kennedy's Decision: Analyzing the Impact on Kennedy's Reputation and the Democratic Party during the Cold War Era

Kennedy's decision to water down the invasion plan had significant political consequences. It not only tarnished his reputation as a strong leader but also impacted the Democratic Party's image during the Cold War era. The failure of the invasion led to questions about Kennedy's ability to handle foreign policy and weakened the party's position in future elections.

The Military Implications: Examining the Strategic Consequences of the Diluted Invasion Plan on the Military Objectives and Outcomes

By diluting the invasion plan, Kennedy compromised the military objectives and outcomes of the operation. The reduced force and limited air support significantly diminished the chances of success. This subchapter explores the strategic consequences of this decision and its impact on the overall outcome of the Bay of Pigs invasion.

Evaluating Kennedy's Leadership Style: Delving into Kennedy's Decision-Making Process and Leadership Style, and Analyzing How it Influenced the Bay of Pigs Invasion

Kennedy's leadership style played a crucial role in shaping the decision-making process leading to the diluted plan. This subchapter analyzes Kennedy's decision-making style, exploring the factors that influenced his choices and the implications it had on the Bay of Pigs invasion.

The Role of Intelligence: Investigating the Intelligence Failures and Shortcomings that Contributed to the Decision to Water Down the Invasion Plan

Intelligence failures and shortcomings significantly impacted the decision to water down the invasion plan. This subchapter delves into the intelligence failures that occurred leading up to the Bay of Pigs invasion, examining how these shortcomings contributed to the decision-making process.

Public Opinion and Media Coverage: Exploring How the Media Covered the Event and the Public's Perception of Kennedy's Decision

The media coverage and public perception of Kennedy's decision to water down the invasion plan played a crucial role in shaping the aftermath of the Bay of Pigs invasion. This subchapter analyzes how the media covered the event and how the public reacted to Kennedy's decision.

The Cuban Exile Community: Analyzing the Impact on the Cuban Exile Community and their Subsequent Role in Anti-Castro Activities

The diluted invasion plan had a profound impact on the Cuban exile community. This subchapter explores the consequences of Kennedy's decision on the Cuban exile community and how it influenced their subsequent role in anti-Castro activities.

Comparing Kennedy's Approach to Previous Administrations: Contrasting Kennedy's Handling of the Bay of Pigs Invasion with Previous Administrations' Policies toward Cuba and the Soviets

By contrasting Kennedy's approach to the Bay of Pigs invasion with previous administrations' policies toward Cuba and the Soviets, this subchapter highlights the unique factors that influenced Kennedy's decision-making process.

International Implications: Examining How Kennedy's Decision Affected US Relations with Other Countries, Particularly in Latin America and the Soviet Union

Kennedy's decision to water down the invasion plan had far-reaching international implications. This subchapter explores how this decision affected US relations with other countries, especially in Latin America and the Soviet Union.

Lessons Learned: Assessing the Long-Term Consequences of Kennedy's Decision and its Impact on Future US Foreign Policy

This subchapter assesses the long-term consequences of Kennedy's decision and its impact on future US foreign policy. By analyzing the lessons learned from the Bay of Pigs invasion, we gain insights into how this event shaped the nation's approach to future foreign affairs.

Conspiracy Theories and Alternate Interpretations: Investigating Conspiracy Theories and Alternative Explanations for Kennedy's Decision to Water Down the Invasion Plan, and their Impact on Historical Interpretations

Finally, this subchapter investigates the conspiracy theories and alternative explanations surrounding Kennedy's decision to water down the invasion plan. By exploring these theories and their impact on historical interpretations, we shed light on the different perspectives and narratives surrounding the Bay of Pigs invasion.

The Influence of Advisory Committees and Military Experts

One of the key factors that contributed to President John F. Kennedy's decision to water down the Bay of Pigs invasion was the influence of advisory committees and military experts. In this subchapter, we will delve into the role played by these individuals and organizations in shaping the outcome of this ill-fated operation.

Kennedy, as a young and relatively inexperienced president, heavily relied on the advice and expertise of his advisors and military officials. These individuals, who were part of various advisory committees, provided valuable insights and recommendations on matters of national security and foreign policy. However, their influence on the Bay of Pigs invasion proved to be detrimental.

The Joint Chiefs of Staff, a group of high-ranking military officers, was tasked with developing and executing the invasion plan. These military experts believed in a full-scale military operation that would swiftly overthrow Fidel Castro's regime. However, Kennedy, fearing Soviet retaliation and a potential escalation of the Cold War, decided to scale back the operation.

The president also sought advice from the 5412 Committee, which was responsible for coordinating covert activities against Cuba. This committee, composed of representatives from various government agencies, recommended a more cautious approach. They argued that a small-scale operation, using Cuban exiles as the main force, would be sufficient to achieve the objective of overthrowing Castro.

The influence of these advisory committees and military experts ultimately influenced Kennedy's decision to approve the diluted invasion plan. Their cautious recommendations and emphasis on avoiding direct conflict with the Soviet Union played a significant role in shaping the outcome of the operation.

However, it is important to note that while Kennedy relied on the advice of these committees and experts, the final decision rested with him. The subchapter will also analyze Kennedy's leadership style and decision-making process, exploring how his personal beliefs and political considerations influenced the Bay of Pigs invasion.

By examining the influence of advisory committees and military experts, historians can gain a deeper understanding of the complex dynamics that led to Kennedy's great mistake. This subchapter will provide valuable insights into the decision-making process and shed light on the political, military, and strategic implications of the diluted invasion plan. It will also contribute to the ongoing debate about the long-term consequences of Kennedy's decision on US foreign policy and the nation's reputation during the Cold War era.

Kennedy's Personal Involvement in the Invasion

President John F. Kennedy's personal involvement in the Bay of Pigs invasion was a crucial factor in the ultimate failure of the mission. This subchapter delves into Kennedy's decision-making process, his leadership style, and how they influenced the outcome of the invasion.

Kennedy, as a young and charismatic leader, faced immense pressure during the Cold War era. With fears of Soviet expansion in the Americas and the rise of communism in Cuba under Fidel Castro, Kennedy was determined to demonstrate strength and resolve in dealing with the perceived threat. However, his decision to water down the invasion plan showcased a hesitant and cautious approach, ultimately leading to disastrous consequences.

In this subchapter, historians will analyze Kennedy's leadership style and its impact on the Bay of Pigs invasion. Kennedy's preference for a consensus-driven decision-making process often resulted in a lack of decisive action. This, combined with his reliance on conflicting advice from advisors, contributed to the diluted invasion plan that was ill-prepared and poorly executed.

Furthermore, the subchapter will explore Kennedy's personal involvement in the decision-making process. Despite his initial reservations about the invasion plan, Kennedy ultimately authorized it, taking personal responsibility for its success. This level of personal involvement distinguishes Kennedy from previous administrations and highlights his desire to maintain control over the operation.

The subchapter will also investigate the role of intelligence in shaping Kennedy's decision-making process. It will explore the intelligence failures and shortcomings that influenced Kennedy's decision to water down the invasion plan. The lack of accurate and reliable intelligence ultimately led to a misinterpretation of the situation on the ground in Cuba, further contributing to the failure of the mission.

Additionally, this subchapter will address the impact of Kennedy's decision on his reputation and the Democratic Party during the Cold War era. The political fallout of the failed invasion tarnished Kennedy's image as a strong leader and raised questions about his ability to handle national security matters. It also tested the loyalty and support of his party, as they had to navigate the aftermath of the failed mission.

Overall, this subchapter aims to provide a comprehensive analysis of Kennedy's personal involvement in the Bay of Pigs invasion. By examining his decision-making process, leadership style, and the various factors that influenced his choices, historians can gain a deeper understanding of the events that unfolded and their long-term consequences on US foreign policy.

Repercussions on Kennedy's Leadership Style in Future Crisis Management

The Bay of Pigs invasion of 1961, orchestrated by President John F. Kennedy, was a significant event in United States history. This subchapter explores the repercussions of Kennedy's leadership style during this crisis and how it shaped future crisis management strategies.

Kennedy's decision to water down the invasion plan for fear of provoking a direct confrontation with the Soviets had profound political fallout. His reputation as a strong and decisive leader was severely tarnished, and the Democratic Party faced criticism for its handling of the Cold War era. Historians have analyzed the impact of this decision on Kennedy's standing both domestically and internationally and its lasting effects on US foreign policy.

The military implications of the diluted invasion plan were significant. By reducing the number of troops and aircraft involved, the strategic objectives of the mission were compromised, leading to a disastrous outcome. This subchapter delves into the consequences of Kennedy's decision on the military objectives and outcomes, shedding light on the shortcomings of his leadership style.

Evaluating Kennedy's leadership style and decision-making process is crucial to understanding the Bay of Pigs invasion. By analyzing his approach to crisis management and how it influenced the outcome, historians can gain insight into his leadership strengths and weaknesses. This subchapter provides a comprehensive examination of Kennedy's decision-making process and its impact on the invasion.

The role of intelligence failures and shortcomings cannot be ignored when discussing the diluted invasion plan. This subchapter investigates the intelligence failures that contributed to the decision to water down the plan. By understanding these shortcomings, historians can paint a clearer picture of the decision-making process and its consequences.

Public opinion and media coverage played a significant role in shaping the perception of Kennedy's decision. This subchapter explores how the media covered the event and the public's perception of Kennedy's leadership style. By analyzing public opinion and media narratives, historians can uncover the impact of the Bay of Pigs invasion on Kennedy's reputation and public trust.

The Cuban exile community also experienced the repercussions of Kennedy's decision. This subchapter analyzes the impact on the Cuban exile community and their subsequent involvement in anti-Castro activities. By studying their role and reactions, historians can understand the long-term consequences of Kennedy's decision on this community.

Comparing Kennedy's approach to previous administrations' policies toward Cuba and the Soviets is crucial for historical analysis. This subchapter contrasts Kennedy's handling of the Bay of Pigs invasion with previous administrations' strategies, highlighting the differences and implications for US foreign policy.

Kennedy's decision also had international implications. This subchapter examines how his choice affected US relations with other countries, particularly in Latin America and the Soviet Union. By understanding these international ramifications, historians can assess the long-term consequences of Kennedy's decision on global politics.

Lastly, conspiracy theories and alternative interpretations of Kennedy's decision are investigated. This subchapter delves into the various theories and interpretations surrounding the watered-down invasion plan and their impact on historical interpretations. By considering alternative explanations, historians can gain a more comprehensive understanding of the events at the Bay of Pigs.

In conclusion, the repercussions of Kennedy's leadership style in future crisis management were far-reaching. This subchapter provides a comprehensive analysis of these consequences, addressing various niches of interest to historians. By examining the political, military, intelligence, public opinion, and international implications, as well as considering the role of the Cuban exile community, comparing Kennedy's approach to previous administrations, and investigating conspiracy theories, historians can unravel the truth behind Kennedy's great mistake and its enduring impact on US history.

Chapter 5: The Role of Intelligence: Investigating the Intelligence Failures and Shortcomings That Contributed to the Decision to Water Down the Invasion Plan

Intelligence Gathering and Analysis Before the Invasion

In the subchapter titled "Intelligence Gathering and Analysis Before the Invasion," we delve into the critical role that intelligence played in shaping the ill-fated Bay of Pigs invasion. Addressing a niche audience of historians, we aim to uncover the truth behind the decision-making process that led to the watering down of the invasion plan. By examining the intelligence failures and shortcomings, we shed light on the factors that contributed to this pivotal moment in Cold War history.

The chapter begins by analyzing the intelligence available to President Kennedy and his advisors prior to the invasion. We scrutinize the sources, methods, and quality of information that influenced their decision-making process. It becomes evident that crucial intelligence was either misinterpreted, overlooked, or dismissed, leading to a flawed understanding of the situation on the ground in Cuba.

Furthermore, we explore the political implications of Kennedy's decision to water down the invasion plan for fear of Soviet intervention. By examining the impact on Kennedy's reputation and the Democratic Party during the Cold War era, we assess the consequences of prioritizing political considerations over military objectives.

The subchapter also delves into the military implications of the diluted invasion plan. We analyze the strategic consequences and outcomes resulting from the decision to scale back the operation. By comparing the original plan to the revised version, we evaluate the extent to which the watering down affected the military's ability to achieve its objectives.

Our analysis extends beyond the immediate consequences, as we explore Kennedy's leadership style in the decision-making process. By examining his approach and its influence on the Bay of Pigs invasion, we gain insight into his leadership capabilities and decision-making style in the face of a complex and high-stakes situation.

Lastly, we investigate the role of intelligence failures and shortcomings in contributing to the decision to water down the invasion plan. By uncovering the intelligence gaps and lapses, we paint a comprehensive picture of the intelligence community's role in the lead-up to the invasion.

In conclusion, this subchapter sheds light on the intelligence gathering and analysis that preceded the Bay of Pigs invasion. By addressing the interests of historians and various niches, we aim to provide a comprehensive understanding of how intelligence failures, political considerations, and leadership style influenced this pivotal moment in Cold War history. Through thorough analysis, we contribute to the ongoing discussion surrounding Kennedy's great mistake and its long-term impact on US foreign policy.

The Failure to Accurately Assess Cuban Defense Capabilities

In the subchapter titled "The Failure to Accurately Assess Cuban Defense Capabilities," we delve into a critical aspect of the Bay of Pigs invasion that has been widely overlooked: the failure to accurately assess Cuban defense capabilities. Addressed to historians, this subchapter aims to shed light on the shortcomings of the intelligence gathered and the implications it had on the overall planning and execution of the invasion.

The Bay of Pigs invasion was intended to overthrow Fidel Castro's regime in Cuba, which posed a significant threat to American interests during the Cold War era. However, a crucial misstep was made in underestimating the strength and preparedness of the Cuban military. This misjudgment ultimately led to the failure of the invasion and had far-reaching consequences.

Through meticulous research and analysis, we uncover the intelligence failures that contributed to this oversight. We examine the sources of information available to President Kennedy and his advisors, including CIA reports, aerial reconnaissance, and human intelligence. Despite these resources, a comprehensive assessment of Cuban defense capabilities was not accurately made, resulting in a misguided belief that the invasion would be swift and successful.

Furthermore, we explore the consequences of this failure. The military implications were profound, as the diluted invasion plan was ill-equipped to counter the Cuban forces. The inability to accurately assess Cuban defense capabilities had strategic consequences, leading to a lack of support from the local population and ultimately the defeat of the invading forces.

Additionally, we analyze Kennedy's leadership style and decision-making process, investigating how these factors influenced the evaluation of Cuban defense capabilities. Did political considerations influence the intelligence analysis? Did Kennedy's desire to avoid direct confrontation with the Soviet Union cloud his judgment? These questions are explored to provide a comprehensive understanding of the decision-making process behind the watered-down invasion plan.

Ultimately, the failure to accurately assess Cuban defense capabilities had far-reaching implications. It affected Kennedy's reputation and the Democratic Party during the Cold War era, as well as US relations with other countries, particularly in Latin America and the Soviet Union. Lessons learned from this failure shaped future US foreign policy decisions, highlighting the importance of accurate intelligence assessment in military planning.

By addressing this overlooked aspect of the Bay of Pigs invasion, we contribute to a more comprehensive understanding of the events that unfolded during this pivotal moment in history. We invite historians to critically analyze the intelligence failures and their impact on the overall outcome of the invasion, considering alternative explanations and conspiracy theories that have emerged over time.

The Overreliance on Questionable Sources

In the realm of historical analysis, it is of utmost importance to rely on credible and verified sources to uncover the truth behind significant events. However, the Bay of Pigs invasion, one of the most notorious episodes in American history, was marred by an overreliance on questionable sources. This subchapter aims to shed light on the detrimental consequences of this reliance, which ultimately led to President John F. Kennedy's ill-fated decision to water down the invasion plan.

From the outset, it is crucial to acknowledge that Kennedy's administration based its decision-making process on flawed intelligence. The Central Intelligence Agency (CIA), responsible for gathering information on Cuba and advising the president, relied heavily on unreliable sources within the Cuban exile community. These exiled individuals, motivated by their desire to overthrow Fidel Castro's regime, often supplied exaggerated or biased information to justify a more aggressive approach.

As historians, we must critically analyze the role of these sources and their impact on the decision-making process. By doing so, we can uncover the extent to which Kennedy's administration was influenced by misinformation and false promises of Cuban support. This exploration allows us to understand the flawed intelligence apparatus that contributed to the dilution of the invasion plan.

Furthermore, the media's coverage of the events surrounding the Bay of Pigs invasion played a significant role in shaping public opinion and, consequently, Kennedy's decision-making process. Journalists, too, relied heavily on these same questionable sources within the Cuban exile community. Consequently, the media perpetuated a narrative that further reinforced the need for a more aggressive approach, thus pushing Kennedy towards the ill-fated decision to water down the invasion plan.

In retrospect, it is evident that Kennedy's overreliance on questionable sources was a pivotal factor in his great mistake. By delving into the flaws within the intelligence community and exploring the media's role in perpetuating this flawed narrative, historians can gain a more nuanced understanding of the events leading up to the Bay of Pigs invasion. This analysis allows us to evaluate the long-term consequences of Kennedy's decision and its impact on future US foreign policy.

Ultimately, by critically examining the overreliance on questionable sources, historians can unveil the truth behind Kennedy's great mistake, shedding new light on this pivotal moment in American history. Through this exploration, we can learn valuable lessons about the importance of robust intelligence gathering, objective media coverage, and the need for a discerning approach when analyzing historical events.

The Impact of Misinterpreted Intelligence on Decision-Making

In the realm of history, few events have sparked as much controversy and speculation as the Bay of Pigs invasion. President John F. Kennedy's decision to water down the operation has long been a subject of intense scrutiny and debate. The consequences of this decision, rooted in the misinterpretation of intelligence, reverberated far beyond the shores of Cuba, shaking the very foundations of American foreign policy.

Historians have long sought to uncover the truth behind Kennedy's great mistake. Central to this quest is an exploration of how misinterpreted intelligence played a pivotal role in shaping the President's decision-making process. The intelligence reports available to Kennedy at the time painted a picture of a Cuban population ripe for rebellion against Fidel Castro's regime. However, these reports failed to take into account crucial factors such as Castro's strong grip on power and the support he enjoyed from the Soviet Union.

This misinterpretation of intelligence led Kennedy to believe that a full-scale invasion, as initially planned, would result in a popular uprising against Castro. Fearing direct confrontation with the Soviet Union, Kennedy made the fateful decision to water down the operation, reducing the number of troops and air support. This critical error in judgment had far-reaching implications.

The impact of misinterpreted intelligence on decision-making cannot be understated. By underestimating Castro's hold on power and misjudging the potential for popular support, Kennedy set the stage for a disastrous outcome. The invasion force, ill-prepared and lacking sufficient resources, was quickly overwhelmed by Castro's forces. The failure of the Bay of Pigs invasion not only led to the capture and imprisonment of over a thousand Cuban exiles but also dealt a severe blow to America's credibility on the international stage.

Moreover, the misinterpretation of intelligence had long-term consequences for US-Soviet relations. The Soviet Union, perceiving

Kennedy's decision as a sign of weakness, became emboldened in their pursuit of expanding influence in Latin America. This led to the Cuban Missile Crisis just a year later, which brought the world to the brink of nuclear war.

As historians delve deeper into the events surrounding Kennedy's great mistake, it becomes clear that the impact of misinterpreted intelligence on decision-making cannot be underestimated. It serves as a cautionary tale, highlighting the need for rigorous analysis and an understanding of the complexities of geopolitical situations. Only through learning from these mistakes can we hope to avoid similar pitfalls in the future, ensuring that history does not repeat itself.

Reforms and Improvements in Intelligence Gathering After the Bay of Pigs

The Bay of Pigs invasion in April 1961 was a pivotal event in American history and had far-reaching consequences for the Kennedy administration, the Cold War era, and US foreign policy. It exposed significant shortcomings in intelligence gathering, leading to a reassessment of intelligence operations and subsequent reforms and improvements.

The failure of the invasion was largely attributed to flawed intelligence assessments that underestimated Cuban military capabilities and the support for Fidel Castro's regime. This intelligence failure resulted in a poorly planned and executed invasion, ultimately leading to the embarrassment and political fallout for President Kennedy and the Democratic Party.

In the aftermath of the Bay of Pigs, the Kennedy administration recognized the urgent need for intelligence reform. The Central Intelligence Agency (CIA) underwent a comprehensive review of its intelligence gathering methods and operations. This led to the implementation of several reforms aimed at improving the accuracy and reliability of intelligence assessments.

One of the key reforms was the establishment of the Office of National Estimates (ONE), which was tasked with providing coordinated and authoritative intelligence assessments to policymakers. This centralized approach aimed to prevent the kind of fragmented intelligence assessments that had contributed to the failure of the Bay of Pigs invasion.

Additionally, the Kennedy administration invested heavily in improving human intelligence capabilities. They recognized the importance of recruiting and training agents with firsthand knowledge of the target countries, including Cuba. This meant that intelligence agencies had a better understanding of the political, military, and social dynamics within Cuba, enabling more accurate assessments and informed decision-making.

Moreover, the Kennedy administration sought to enhance intelligence sharing and cooperation with international partners. They realized that the Bay of Pigs invasion had exposed the limitations of relying solely on American intelligence resources. By working closely with allies and sharing intelligence, they could access a broader range of information and perspectives, thereby improving the quality and reliability of intelligence assessments.

These reforms and improvements in intelligence gathering after the Bay of Pigs invasion had a profound impact on US foreign policy. They helped prevent similar intelligence failures in future operations and provided policymakers with more accurate and reliable information to inform their decisions. The lessons learned from the Bay of Pigs invasion led to a more sophisticated and effective intelligence apparatus, which played a crucial role in shaping American policies during the Cold War era and beyond.

In conclusion, the Bay of Pigs invasion was a wake-up call for the Kennedy administration, highlighting the need for significant reforms and improvements in intelligence gathering. The establishment of the Office of National Estimates, the enhancement of human intelligence capabilities, and the emphasis on international cooperation were pivotal in preventing future intelligence failures. These reforms had a lasting impact on US foreign policy and ensured that the mistakes made during the Bay of Pigs invasion would not be repeated.

Chapter 6: Public Opinion and Media Coverage: Exploring How the Media Covered the Event and the Public's Perception of Kennedy's Decision

Media Coverage Leading up to the Invasion

The media played a crucial role in shaping public opinion and influencing the events leading up to the Bay of Pigs invasion. As tensions between the United States and the Soviet Union continued to escalate during the Cold War era, President John F. Kennedy found himself facing a difficult decision regarding Cuba and its communist leader, Fidel Castro. The media coverage leading up to the invasion provides valuable insights into the political climate and public perception of Kennedy's decision-making process.

In the months preceding the invasion, the media focused heavily on the growing threat of communism in Cuba. Newspapers, magazines, and television broadcasts provided extensive coverage of Castro's regime and its alignment with the Soviet Union. This coverage created a sense of urgency among the American public and fueled fears of a communist stronghold just 90 miles off the coast of Florida.

However, as Kennedy deliberated on the best course of action, the media's coverage began to shift. Rumors of a potential invasion of Cuba started to circulate, and journalists sought to uncover the truth behind these speculations. The media's scrutiny intensified as Kennedy's administration carefully managed the flow of information to maintain secrecy and avoid public backlash.

As the invasion plan was formulated, the media's coverage became more intense. Journalists sought to uncover the details of the operation, often relying on anonymous sources within the government or leaks from disgruntled officials. However, the Kennedy administration's efforts to control the narrative limited the information available to the media, resulting in a lack of comprehensive reporting on the invasion plan.

On the eve of the invasion, the media's coverage intensified further. Speculations and rumors ran rampant, as journalists and commentators attempted to piece together the puzzle of the impending military operation. However, due to the limited information available, the media's coverage was often speculative and lacked concrete facts.

Overall, the media coverage leading up to the Bay of Pigs invasion played a significant role in shaping public opinion and fueling the narrative surrounding Kennedy's decision-making process. The media's focus on communism, their attempts to uncover the truth behind the invasion plan, and their speculations on the eve of the operation all contributed to the political fallout and the subsequent impact on Kennedy's reputation and the Democratic Party during the Cold War era.

For historians examining this period, the media coverage provides valuable insights into the challenges faced by Kennedy and his administration, as well as the public's perception of their decisions. It also highlights the role of the media as a powerful agent in shaping historical events and public opinion.

The Media's Reaction to the Watered-Down Invasion Plan

In the subchapter titled "The Media's Reaction to the Watered-Down Invasion Plan" of the book "Kennedy's Great Mistake: Unveiling the Truth Behind the Watered-Down Bay of Pigs Invasion," we delve into the role of the media and its coverage of the event. This chapter is particularly relevant to historians and those interested in understanding the public perception of Kennedy's decision during the Cold War era.

The media played a crucial role in shaping public opinion and disseminating information about the Bay of Pigs invasion. As news of the watered-down invasion plan emerged, journalists, both domestic and international, were quick to scrutinize Kennedy's decision-making process. Their analysis focused on the potential political fallout, military implications, and the role of intelligence failures in the diluted invasion plan.

Newspapers across the United States and around the world published headlines expressing disappointment, confusion, and even outrage at Kennedy's handling of the situation. The media questioned Kennedy's leadership style and his ability to make sound decisions in the face of Soviet aggression. Critics argued that the watered-down invasion plan showcased weakness and indecisiveness, undermining Kennedy's reputation as a strong leader.

Television news programs also played a significant role in shaping public opinion. The images of captured Cuban exiles and the failed invasion attempt were broadcasted widely, further intensifying the negative perception of Kennedy's decision. The media's coverage of the event influenced public sentiment, leading to a decline in Kennedy's approval ratings and a backlash against the Democratic Party.

Moreover, the media's portrayal of the Cuban exile community and their subsequent role in anti-Castro activities added a layer of complexity to the narrative. Journalists highlighted the disillusionment and anger within the Cuban exile community, who felt betrayed by Kennedy's decision. This coverage shed light on the impact of the watered-down invasion plan on the Cuban exile community and its subsequent involvement in anti-Castro activities.

The media's reaction to the watered-down invasion plan also had international implications. It affected US relations with other countries, particularly in Latin America and the Soviet Union. The media coverage amplified international skepticism and criticism of Kennedy's decision, damaging America's credibility and reputation.

This chapter explores the media's role in shaping public opinion and analyzing the consequences of Kennedy's decision. By examining news articles, television broadcasts, and public reactions, historians gain a comprehensive understanding of how the media covered the event and its impact on historical interpretations. The subchapter provides valuable insights into the media's influence on public perception, the political fallout, and the international implications of Kennedy's decision during the Cold War era.

Public Opinion Polls and Surveys

Public opinion plays a crucial role in shaping political decisions and understanding the impact of historical events. In the case of the Bay of Pigs invasion, public opinion and media coverage had a significant influence on President Kennedy's decision-making process and the subsequent fallout from that decision. This subchapter delves into the public's perception of Kennedy's decision and the role of media in shaping that perception.

Public opinion polls conducted during the Cold War era revealed a mixed response to Kennedy's handling of the Bay of Pigs invasion. While some Americans supported the president's decision to water down the invasion plan for fear of Soviet retaliation, others criticized it as a sign of weakness and appeasement. These polls provide valuable insights into the diverse viewpoints held by the American public at the time.

The media's coverage of the event also played a crucial role in shaping public opinion. Newspapers, TV news, and radio broadcasts provided extensive coverage of the invasion and its aftermath. Journalists brought forth different interpretations of Kennedy's decision, highlighting both the strategic considerations and the political implications. Some media outlets portrayed Kennedy as a wise leader who prioritized avoiding a potential nuclear war, while others labeled him as indecisive and inexperienced.

The subchapter will explore how the media covered the event, analyzing the biases, perspectives, and narratives presented. It will also examine the ways in which the public's perception of Kennedy's decision was influenced by media coverage. Moreover, it will consider the long-term impact of the media's portrayal of the Bay of Pigs invasion on Kennedy's reputation and the Democratic Party during the Cold War era.

Additionally, this subchapter will investigate how public opinion and media coverage affected the Cuban exile community. The Cuban exiles had high hopes for the Bay of Pigs invasion, expecting a swift overthrow of Fidel Castro's regime. However, Kennedy's decision to water down the invasion plan resulted in a failed operation, leading to disillusionment among the exiles. The subchapter will analyze the impact of this event on the Cuban exile community and its subsequent role in anti-Castro activities.

In conclusion, public opinion polls and media coverage played a pivotal role in shaping the perception of Kennedy's decision to water down the Bay of Pigs invasion. Understanding the public's response, media narratives, and their impact on various stakeholders provides valuable insights into the political fallout, the military implications, and Kennedy's leadership style during this critical period of the Cold War era. By examining these aspects, historians can gain a comprehensive understanding of the historical significance and consequences of Kennedy's great mistake.

The Impact of Media Coverage on Kennedy's Image

The media has always played a crucial role in shaping public opinion and influencing the perception of political leaders. In the case of President John F. Kennedy and the Bay of Pigs invasion, media coverage had a significant impact on Kennedy's image both domestically and internationally.

The media coverage of the Bay of Pigs invasion was intense and widespread. Journalists from various outlets covered the event, providing daily updates and analysis of the situation. Their reporting focused not only on the failure of the invasion but also on the perceived incompetence of the Kennedy administration. Headlines such as "Kennedy's Great Mistake" and "Watered-Down Invasion Plan" dominated the news, creating a negative narrative around Kennedy's decision-making.

The media's portrayal of Kennedy's handling of the Bay of Pigs invasion had several consequences. Firstly, it damaged Kennedy's reputation as a strong and capable leader. The public began to question his judgment and ability to handle national security issues. This perception was further exacerbated by comparisons to previous administrations' policies towards Cuba and the Soviets. Kennedy's reputation as a Cold War warrior took a hit, and his credibility as a leader was questioned.

Secondly, the media coverage of the Bay of Pigs invasion had political implications. The Democratic Party, already facing challenges during the Cold War era, suffered a blow to its reputation. Many within the party criticized Kennedy's decision, leading to internal divisions and a loss of trust among party members. Kennedy's weakened position within his own party made it difficult for him to push forward his domestic and foreign policy agenda.

Internationally, the media coverage of the Bay of Pigs invasion had implications for US relations with other countries, particularly in Latin America and the Soviet Union. The perceived failure of the invasion and the negative portrayal of Kennedy's leadership style damaged the United States' image as a global superpower. This weakened position opened the door for increased Soviet influence in Latin America and strained relations between the United States and the Soviet Union.

In conclusion, the media coverage of the Bay of Pigs invasion had a profound impact on Kennedy's image. It damaged his reputation as a strong leader, weakened the Democratic Party, and strained US relations with other countries. The negative narrative created by the media coverage of the event continues to shape historical interpretations of Kennedy's presidency. Understanding the role of media in shaping public opinion is crucial for historians analyzing Kennedy's great mistake and its consequences.

Historical Interpretations of Media Influence on the Bay of Pigs

The Bay of Pigs invasion, a pivotal event during the Cold War era, has been the subject of extensive historical analysis. One aspect that has received significant attention is the role of media in shaping public perception and influencing the outcome of the invasion. This subchapter delves into the historical interpretations of media influence on the Bay of Pigs, examining the various perspectives and arguments put forward by historians.

One widely discussed interpretation is that the media played a crucial role in exposing the flaws and failures of the invasion plan. Journalists, armed with information and access to sources, provided critical analysis and coverage that shed light on the misguided decision-making and strategic miscalculations. This interpretation asserts that without the media's scrutiny, the true extent of Kennedy's mistake would not have been fully revealed to the public and the Democratic Party.

On the other hand, some historians argue that the media's coverage of the Bay of Pigs invasion was biased and sensationalized. They believe that the media exaggerated the failures of the invasion, leading to a tarnished reputation for Kennedy and the Democratic Party. This interpretation suggests that the media's portrayal of the event was driven by political motivations and a desire to undermine Kennedy's leadership.

Moreover, historians have explored the impact of media coverage on the Cuban exile community. Some argue that the media's portrayal of the invasion as a failure and the subsequent lack of US support for the exiles created disillusionment and a sense of betrayal within the community. This interpretation emphasizes the long-term consequences of media influence on the Cuban exile community's subsequent involvement in anti-Castro activities.

Conspiracy theories and alternate interpretations have also emerged regarding the media's role in the Bay of Pigs. Some historians propose that the media was manipulated by the US government to shape public opinion. They contend that the media's coverage was deliberately crafted to justify Kennedy's decision to water down the invasion plan.

In conclusion, the historical interpretations of media influence on the Bay of Pigs invasion vary, reflecting the complexity of the event and its implications. While some argue that the media played a crucial role in exposing the flaws of the invasion plan, others contend that the media's coverage was biased and sensationalized. The impact of media coverage on the Cuban exile community and the emergence of conspiracy theories further contribute to the diverse interpretations. By examining these different perspectives, historians can gain a deeper understanding of the multifaceted nature of the Bay of Pigs invasion and its historical significance.

Chapter 7: The Cuban Exile Community: Analyzing the Impact on the Cuban Exile Community and Their Subsequent Role in Anti-Castro Activities

The Cuban Exile Community Before the Bay of Pigs

Before delving into the intricacies of the Bay of Pigs invasion and its watered-down plan, it is essential to first understand the crucial role played by the Cuban exile community. This subchapter aims to explore the impact of the Cuban exile community and their subsequent role in anti-Castro activities.

The Cuban exile community, consisting of individuals who fled Cuba following Fidel Castro's rise to power in 1959, was a significant force during this period. These exiles were deeply rooted in their desire to overthrow Castro's regime and reclaim their homeland. Many of them had experienced firsthand the oppressive policies and human rights violations under Castro's rule. Consequently, they were determined to take action and actively sought support from the United States to aid their cause.

The exile community, buoyed by their passion and conviction, lobbied extensively to garner support among the American public and policymakers. They became a prominent voice, advocating for a more aggressive stance against Castro's communist regime. Their influence reached the highest echelons of power, with key members of the community engaging directly with President John F. Kennedy and his administration.

The Cuban exile community's strong ties to the CIA and their knowledge of Cuba's internal dynamics made them invaluable assets in planning the Bay of Pigs invasion. Their intimate understanding of the terrain, language, and cultural nuances provided critical insights to the intelligence community. The exiles also played a vital role in recruiting and training the Cuban Brigade 2506, the force that would ultimately carry out the invasion.

However, despite their enthusiasm and dedication, the Cuban exile community faced challenges in gaining full support for their desired military intervention. Some members of the Kennedy administration, particularly those concerned about the potential escalation of the conflict and Soviet retaliation, were hesitant to fully embrace their recommendations.

The subsequent decision by Kennedy and his advisors to water down the invasion plan had a profound impact on the Cuban exile community. They felt betrayed and disheartened, believing that their cause had been sacrificed for political expediency. This disillusionment fueled a strong sense of resentment and a desire to take matters into their own hands.

The Cuban exile community's subsequent role in anti-Castro activities, such as infiltrating Cuba and engaging in covert operations, became a defining feature of their struggle against the Castro regime. Many exiles continued their fight long after the Bay of Pigs, contributing to subsequent efforts to undermine Castro's rule.

In conclusion, the Cuban exile community played a crucial role in the lead-up to the Bay of Pigs invasion. Their passion, knowledge, and determination shaped the course of events and influenced the planning process. The subsequent decision to water down the invasion plan had a lasting impact on the community, fueling their resolve to continue the fight against Castro. Understanding their role is essential in comprehending the full scope of the Bay of Pigs invasion and its aftermath.

The Cuban Exile Community's Expectations and Support

The Cuban exile community played a pivotal role in the events leading up to and following the Bay of Pigs invasion. As the invasion plan took shape, their expectations and support were instrumental in shaping the course of action taken by the Kennedy administration.

For the Cuban exile community, the invasion represented a glimmer of hope in their struggle against Fidel Castro's regime. Many exiles had fled Cuba following Castro's rise to power, leaving behind their homes, businesses, and loved ones. They had long dreamed of returning to a free and democratic Cuba, and the Bay of Pigs invasion seemed to offer them that chance.

Their support for the invasion was unwavering. They provided vital intelligence to the CIA, helping to identify targets and gather information on Castro's forces. They also served as a source of motivation and inspiration for the fighters involved in the operation. The exiles saw themselves not only as liberators but also as representatives of the Cuban people, fighting for their rights and freedom.

However, the expectations of the Cuban exile community were not met. The decision by the Kennedy administration to water down the invasion plan had significant implications for the exiles. The lack of air support and the failure to mobilize a larger force meant that the invasion was doomed from the start. The exiles felt betrayed by the US government, which had promised them support and assistance.

The impact on the Cuban exile community was profound. Many exiles lost their lives or were captured and imprisoned by Castro's forces. The failure of the invasion shattered their hopes and dreams of a free Cuba. It also created a divide within the community, with some questioning the leadership and decision-making of the Kennedy administration.

In the years following the Bay of Pigs invasion, the Cuban exile community became even more determined to oust Castro and restore democracy in Cuba. They organized anti-Castro activities, including sabotage and covert operations, in an attempt to undermine the regime. The exiles became a powerful force in the fight against communism, drawing attention to the plight of the Cuban people and advocating for a tougher stance against Castro's regime.

The Cuban exile community's expectations and support for the Bay of Pigs invasion were instrumental in shaping the events that unfolded. Their unwavering commitment to the cause of a free Cuba, despite the failure of the invasion, demonstrated their resilience and determination. The impact of their support and subsequent actions cannot be understated, as they continued to play a significant role in anti-Castro activities and in shaping US policy towards Cuba in the years to come.

The Disillusionment and Fallout Among Exiles

The Bay of Pigs invasion was a pivotal event during the Cold War era, and its aftermath had far-reaching consequences on various aspects. One significant repercussion was the disillusionment and fallout among the Cuban exiles who had fervently supported and participated in the mission. This subchapter delves into the impact on the Cuban exile community and their subsequent role in anti-Castro activities.

The Cuban exiles had long yearned for the overthrow of Fidel Castro's regime, and the Bay of Pigs invasion was seen as their opportunity to reclaim their homeland. However, when President John F. Kennedy decided to water down the invasion plan, it resulted in a disastrous failure. The exiles felt betrayed and abandoned by the very government they had trusted to support their cause.

The fallout among the exiles was immense. Many felt a deep sense of disillusionment and resentment towards the Kennedy administration. They believed that their sacrifices and efforts had been in vain, and their hopes for a free Cuba shattered. The lack of support from the United States left them demoralized and disheartened.

Despite the setback, the Cuban exiles did not give up. Instead, they channeled their disappointment into a renewed determination to overthrow Castro's regime. They became more active in anti-Castro activities, organizing and supporting various covert operations aimed at destabilizing the Cuban government. The failed Bay of Pigs invasion served as a catalyst for their continued struggle against the communist regime.

The disillusionment and fallout among the exiles also had broader implications. It strained the relationship between the Cuban exile community and the Democratic Party, which had been seen as their political ally. Many exiles turned their backs on the Democrats, feeling betrayed by the party they had once supported. This political fallout had long-lasting effects on the reputation of President Kennedy and the Democratic Party during the Cold War era.

In conclusion, the disillusionment and fallout among the Cuban exiles following the watered-down Bay of Pigs invasion had significant ramifications. It sparked a renewed determination among the exiles to overthrow Castro's regime and strained their relationship with the Democratic Party. The consequences of Kennedy's great mistake were not limited to the military and political realm but also deeply impacted the Cuban exile community and their subsequent actions in anti-Castro activities. This chapter sheds light on the profound and lasting effects of the failed invasion on the Cuban exiles and their role in the ongoing struggle for a free Cuba.

The Cuban Exile Community's Continued Resistance Efforts

The Cuban Exile Community's Continued Resistance Efforts is a subchapter in the book "Kennedy's Great Mistake: Unveiling the Truth Behind the Watered-Down Bay of Pigs Invasion." This subchapter specifically explores the impact of Kennedy's decision on the Cuban exile community and their subsequent role in anti-Castro activities.

The Cuban exile community had long been a vocal and active force against Fidel Castro's regime. Many exiles had fled to the United States seeking refuge and were determined to overthrow the communist government in Cuba. The Bay of Pigs invasion was seen as a golden opportunity for them to regain control of their homeland.

However, when Kennedy decided to water down the invasion plan, it was a devastating blow to the morale and hopes of the Cuban exile community. They had expected full support and assistance from the United States, but instead, they were left to fight an uphill battle with limited resources and inadequate planning.

Despite this setback, the Cuban exile community did not give up. They remained resilient and resourceful, finding alternative ways to oppose Castro's regime. Many exiles joined anti-Castro organizations, such as the Cuban Democratic Revolutionary Front, and continued their fight through political activism, propaganda campaigns, and even acts of sabotage.

One of the most significant resistance efforts was Operation Mongoose, a covert operation launched by the CIA in collaboration with the exile community. Its aim was to destabilize Castro's government through various means, including assassinations, sabotage, and psychological warfare.

Although the Cuban exile community's efforts did not immediately lead to the overthrow of Castro's regime, they played a crucial role in keeping the anti-Castro movement alive. Their determination and perseverance inspired others to join the cause and kept the pressure on the Cuban government.

Moreover, the Cuban exile community's continued resistance efforts had wider implications beyond Cuba. They served as a symbol of resistance against communism and inspired similar movements in other Latin American countries. The exiles' stories and experiences also shaped public opinion and influenced US foreign policy towards Cuba and the Soviet Union during the Cold War era.

In conclusion, despite the disappointment caused by Kennedy's decision to water down the Bay of Pigs invasion, the Cuban exile community did not surrender. They continued their resistance efforts through various means, playing a significant role in the anti-Castro movement. Their determination and resilience had a lasting impact on US foreign policy and inspired similar movements in Latin America.

The Long-Term Relationship Between the Cuban Exile Community and U.S. Government

The Bay of Pigs invasion was a pivotal moment in the history of US-Cuba relations and the Cold War era. One of the lasting legacies of this ill-fated mission was the impact it had on the Cuban exile community and their relationship with the US government.

The Cuban exile community, consisting of individuals who had fled Cuba following Fidel Castro's rise to power, played a crucial role in the planning and execution of the Bay of Pigs invasion. Many of them had been vocal critics of Castro's regime and saw the invasion as an opportunity to overthrow him and restore democracy in Cuba. They provided valuable intelligence, resources, and manpower to the operation.

However, when President John F. Kennedy decided to water down the invasion plan for fear of Soviet intervention, it had profound consequences for the Cuban exile community. The failure of the mission not only shattered their hopes of returning to a free Cuba but also exposed them to retaliation and persecution from Castro's regime. Many were imprisoned, tortured, or forced into exile once again.

The betrayal felt by the Cuban exile community towards the US government was palpable. They believed that the US had abandoned them and prioritized its own interests over the liberation of Cuba. This strained their long-term relationship with the US government and led to a deep sense of mistrust.

In the years following the Bay of Pigs invasion, the Cuban exile community became even more determined to overthrow Castro and supported various anti-Castro activities. They formed organizations, raised funds, and lobbied the US government for support. This activism continued for decades and became a defining characteristic of the Cuban exile community.

The US government, on its part, recognized the value of the Cuban exile community as a political and strategic asset. They provided financial aid, training, and support to the exiles, albeit covertly. This relationship endured even as subsequent administrations adopted different approaches towards Cuba and the Soviets.

Overall, the Bay of Pigs invasion had a profound and lasting impact on the Cuban exile community. It shaped their identity, fueled their activism, and strained their relationship with the US government. The long-term consequences of this relationship are still felt today, as the Cuban exile community continues to play a significant role in shaping US foreign policy towards Cuba.

Chapter 8: Comparing Kennedy's Approach to Previous Administrations: Contrasting Kennedy's Handling of the Bay of Pigs

Invasion with Previous Administrations' Policies Toward Cuba and the Soviets

The Eisenhower Administration's Approach to Cuba

During the Eisenhower administration, the United States adopted a strong anti-communist stance towards Cuba, which would ultimately shape President Kennedy's approach to the island nation. Under Eisenhower's leadership, the United States began implementing a series of economic and political measures to isolate Cuba and undermine Fidel Castro's regime.

One of the key strategies employed by the Eisenhower administration was the imposition of economic sanctions. In 1960, the United States placed an embargo on all trade with Cuba, cutting off its main source of economic support. This move was intended to weaken Castro's government and force him to abandon his communist agenda. Additionally, the administration sought to isolate Cuba diplomatically by pressuring other countries to sever their ties with the Castro regime.

Furthermore, the Eisenhower administration also supported covert operations aimed at destabilizing Castro's government. The Central Intelligence Agency (CIA) began training and arming Cuban exiles with the goal of overthrowing Castro. These efforts culminated in the ill-fated Bay of Pigs invasion, which was initially planned and authorized during Eisenhower's tenure but executed under Kennedy.

The Eisenhower administration took a hardline approach towards Cuba due to its close proximity to the United States and the perceived threat of communism spreading in the region. The administration feared that if left unchecked, Castro's regime could become a Soviet ally, posing a direct threat to U.S. national security.

This aggressive stance towards Cuba set the stage for President Kennedy's handling of the Bay of Pigs invasion. Kennedy, who inherited the operation from Eisenhower, faced a difficult decision - whether to proceed with the original invasion plan or adopt a more cautious approach. Ultimately, Kennedy chose to water down the invasion plan due to concerns about escalating tensions with the Soviet Union.

This decision had far-reaching consequences, both politically and militarily. Politically, Kennedy's reputation suffered a blow, as many perceived his decision as weak and indecisive. The Democratic Party also faced significant backlash, as the failure of the invasion was seen as a reflection of the party's inability to effectively deal with the communist threat.

From a military standpoint, the diluted invasion plan had strategic implications. The initial plan called for a larger force and more extensive air support, but the scaled-down version lacked the necessary firepower to achieve its objectives. As a result, the invasion was a failure, and the Cuban exile community faced harsh reprisals from Castro's government.

The Eisenhower administration's approach to Cuba, characterized by economic sanctions, covert operations, and diplomatic isolation, set the stage for the Bay of Pigs invasion and ultimately influenced Kennedy's decision-making process. Understanding this context is crucial in analyzing the political, military, and international implications of Kennedy's handling of the invasion. It also sheds light on the role of intelligence failures, media coverage, and the long-term consequences of Kennedy's decision, which continue to be subjects of debate among historians.

Kennedy's Shift in Policy and Rhetoric

In this subchapter, titled "Kennedy's Shift in Policy and Rhetoric," we delve into President John F. Kennedy's decision to water down the Bay of Pigs invasion and its far-reaching implications. Historians interested in understanding the intricacies of this critical moment in American history will find this analysis enlightening.

One of the primary focuses of this subchapter is to examine the political fallout of Kennedy's decision. By watering down the invasion plan for fear of the Soviets, Kennedy inadvertently tarnished his reputation and that of the Democratic Party during the Cold War era. We will delve into the public's perception of Kennedy's decision and how it affected his leadership style and decision-making process.

Furthermore, it is essential to understand the military implications of the diluted invasion plan. By examining the strategic consequences and outcomes, we gain valuable insights into the effectiveness of Kennedy's approach. This analysis will shed light on the military objectives and the long-term impact on future US foreign policy.

Another crucial aspect we will explore is the role of intelligence in the decision-making process. Investigating the intelligence failures and shortcomings that contributed to the decision to water down the invasion plan provides a comprehensive understanding of the factors at play.

Additionally, this subchapter examines the media coverage and public opinion surrounding the Bay of Pigs invasion. By exploring how the media covered the event and the public's perception of Kennedy's decision, we gain insights into the broader implications of this critical moment in history.

Furthermore, we will analyze the impact on the Cuban exile community and their subsequent role in anti-Castro activities. Understanding how Kennedy's decision affected this community is essential in comprehending the complex dynamics of the era.

Comparisons will also be made between Kennedy's approach and that of previous administrations. Contrasting Kennedy's handling of the Bay of Pigs invasion with previous policies toward Cuba and the Soviets provides valuable insights into the evolution of US foreign policy.

Moreover, we will examine the international implications of Kennedy's decision, particularly in Latin America and the Soviet Union. By exploring how Kennedy's decision affected US relations with other countries, we gain a broader perspective on the global impact of this critical moment in history.

Finally, we will assess the long-term consequences of Kennedy's decision and its impact on future US foreign policy. Furthermore, we will investigate conspiracy theories and alternative explanations for Kennedy's decision to water down the invasion plan, as well as their impact on historical interpretations.

Overall, "Kennedy's Shift in Policy and Rhetoric" offers historians a comprehensive analysis of the Bay of Pigs invasion, providing insights into the political, military, intelligence, and international dimensions of this critical moment in American history.

The Bay of Pigs as a Departure from Previous Strategies

In this subchapter titled "The Bay of Pigs as a Departure from Previous Strategies," we delve into the pivotal moment in American history when President John F. Kennedy made the fateful decision to water down the Bay of Pigs invasion plan. This decision marked a significant departure from previous strategies employed by the United States in dealing with the threat of communism, particularly in Latin America.

The Bay of Pigs invasion was initially conceived as a bold and decisive military operation aimed at overthrowing Fidel Castro's communist regime in Cuba. However, under pressure from his advisors and fearing a direct confrontation with the Soviet Union, Kennedy chose a more cautious and restrained approach. This marked a departure from the aggressive policies pursued by previous administrations, such as the Eisenhower and Truman administrations, in their efforts to contain communism.

By diluting the invasion plan, Kennedy hoped to minimize the risk of a nuclear confrontation with the Soviet Union, which had placed missiles in Cuba. However, this decision had far-reaching consequences. Firstly, it severely damaged Kennedy's reputation as a strong leader, both domestically and internationally. Many historians argue that this decision weakened the Democratic Party during the Cold War era, as it appeared to be hesitant and indecisive in the face of communist aggression.

Furthermore, the diluted invasion plan had significant military implications. It compromised the strategic objectives and outcomes of the operation, resulting in a disastrous failure. The lack of air support, inadequate intelligence, and limited resources led to the defeat of the Cuban exile forces, further highlighting the flawed decision-making process.

In evaluating Kennedy's leadership style, we analyze how his decision-making process and leadership influenced the Bay of Pigs invasion. This includes an examination of his reliance on advisors, his preference for consensus-building, and his tendency to prioritize political considerations over military objectives.

Moreover, we investigate the role of intelligence failures and shortcomings that contributed to the decision to water down the invasion plan. This involves a critical analysis of the intelligence community's assessments and the information available to Kennedy at the time.

The subchapter also explores the impact of the Bay of Pigs invasion on public opinion and media coverage. We delve into how the media covered the event and the public's perception of Kennedy's decision. Additionally, we analyze the repercussions on the Cuban exile community and their subsequent role in anti-Castro activities.

Comparing Kennedy's approach to previous administrations, we contrast his handling of the Bay of Pigs invasion with the policies pursued by his predecessors. This includes an examination of the Eisenhower administration's covert operations and the Truman administration's containment policies.

Furthermore, we examine the international implications of Kennedy's decision, particularly in relation to US relations with other countries, especially in Latin America and the Soviet Union. This includes an analysis of how the decision affected US credibility and influence in the region.

Lastly, we assess the long-term consequences of Kennedy's decision and its impact on future US foreign policy. This includes an evaluation of the lessons learned from the Bay of Pigs invasion and how it shaped subsequent approaches to communism and national security.

Additionally, we investigate conspiracy theories and alternative explanations for Kennedy's decision to water down the invasion plan. We analyze the impact of these theories on historical interpretations and the ongoing debate surrounding the Bay of Pigs invasion.

In conclusion, this subchapter provides a comprehensive analysis of the Bay of Pigs invasion as a departure from previous strategies employed by the United States. It examines the political, military, leadership, intelligence, public opinion, and international implications of Kennedy's decision, shedding light on the factors that influenced this critical moment in history.

Historical Comparisons and Evaluations

In this subchapter of "Kennedy's Great Mistake: Unveiling the Truth Behind the Watered-Down Bay of Pigs Invasion," we delve into the various aspects and consequences of President John F. Kennedy's decision to dilute the Bay of Pigs invasion plan. Addressed to historians and those interested in the niches surrounding Kennedy's decision, this chapter aims to provide a comprehensive analysis of the historical comparisons and evaluations related to this pivotal event during the Cold War era.

We begin by examining Kennedy's motivation to water down the invasion plan for fear of the Soviets, comparing it to previous administrations' policies toward Cuba and the Soviets. By contrasting Kennedy's approach with that of his predecessors, we can assess the effectiveness and implications of his decision.

Next, we analyze the political fallout of Kennedy's decision, focusing on its impact on his reputation and the Democratic Party during the Cold War era. This evaluation allows us to understand the long-term consequences of this event on both Kennedy's leadership and the Democratic Party's standing.

Moving forward, we evaluate the military implications of the diluted invasion plan. By examining the strategic consequences and outcomes of this decision, we can uncover the extent to which it affected the military objectives and overall outcome of the Bay of Pigs invasion.

Furthermore, we delve into Kennedy's leadership style and decision-making process, evaluating how it influenced the Bay of Pigs invasion. By studying his leadership style, we can gain insights into the factors that shaped his decision and its subsequent impact.

The role of intelligence is also investigated, with a focus on the failures and shortcomings that contributed to the decision to water down the invasion plan. This evaluation allows us to understand the intelligence landscape at the time and its influence on the outcome of the invasion.

Additionally, we explore the media coverage and public opinion surrounding the event, analyzing how the media covered the event and the public's perception of Kennedy's decision. This evaluation sheds light on the role of media in shaping historical interpretations.

We also analyze the impact on the Cuban exile community and their subsequent role in anti-Castro activities. By assessing the consequences on the Cuban exile community, we can understand their motivations and actions following the diluted invasion plan.

Examining the international implications, we investigate how Kennedy's decision affected US relations with other countries, particularly in Latin America and the Soviet Union. This evaluation allows us to understand the broader impact of this decision on the global stage.

Finally, we assess the long-term consequences of Kennedy's decision and its impact on future US foreign policy. By analyzing the lessons learned from this event, we can gain insights into how it shaped subsequent decision-making processes in US foreign policy.

Furthermore, we investigate conspiracy theories and alternate interpretations surrounding Kennedy's decision to water down the invasion plan. By exploring these alternative explanations, we can uncover the impact they have had on historical interpretations.

Overall, this subchapter provides a comprehensive evaluation of the historical comparisons and evaluations related to Kennedy's decision to dilute the Bay of Pigs invasion plan. By examining the various aspects and consequences, we aim to shed light on the truth behind this pivotal event in Cold War history.

The Impact on U.S.-Cuba Relations Moving Forward

The decision to water down the Bay of Pigs invasion had a profound impact on U.S.-Cuba relations moving forward. This subchapter aims to explore the various aspects of this impact, shedding light on the consequences of Kennedy's great mistake.

One of the most significant consequences of Kennedy's decision was the deterioration of U.S.-Cuba relations. The failed invasion not only solidified Fidel Castro's grip on power but also pushed Cuba further into the arms of the Soviet Union. With the failed attempt to overthrow Castro, the U.S. lost an opportunity to establish a pro-American government in Cuba, and instead, Cuba became a staunch ally of the Soviet Union, heightening tensions between the two superpowers during the Cold War era.

The political fallout of Kennedy's decision was also severe. His reputation suffered a blow, as he was seen as weak and indecisive. Critics argued that he succumbed to the fear of Soviet retaliation, compromising American values and interests in the process. This weakened his position both domestically and internationally, with many questioning his ability to lead during such a critical period of the Cold War.

From a military perspective, the diluted invasion plan had strategic consequences. By reducing the scope and firepower of the invasion force, the U.S. failed to achieve its military objectives, resulting in a resounding defeat. This failure highlighted the shortcomings and limitations of U.S. military capabilities, ultimately leading to a reassessment of military strategies and objectives.

Kennedy's decision-making process and leadership style also came under scrutiny. His reluctance to fully commit to the invasion plan, influenced by his cautious and deliberative approach, had a direct impact on the outcome of the Bay of Pigs invasion. This raised questions about his ability to make tough decisions and effectively lead in times of crisis.

Furthermore, the intelligence failures and shortcomings that contributed to the decision to water down the invasion plan were significant. The CIA's flawed assessment of the situation in Cuba and its overconfidence in the Cuban exile force led to a misguided plan that ultimately doomed the operation. This highlighted the need for reform and improvement in intelligence gathering and analysis.

The impact on the Cuban exile community cannot be understated. Many exiles had put their hopes in the invasion as a means to overthrow Castro and return to their homeland. The failure of the invasion left them disillusioned and marginalized, leading some to engage in anti-Castro activities and fueling a sense of resentment towards the U.S. government.

Kennedy's handling of the Bay of Pigs invasion also contrasted with previous administrations' policies toward Cuba and the Soviets. The failure of the invasion highlighted the shortcomings of the U.S. approach, leading to a reevaluation of strategies and policies towards Cuba and the Soviet Union.

Internationally, Kennedy's decision affected U.S. relations with other countries, particularly in Latin America and the Soviet Union. The failed invasion undermined U.S. credibility and influence in the region, bolstering anti-American sentiment and pushing countries closer to the Soviet sphere of influence.

The long-term consequences of Kennedy's decision were far-reaching. It reshaped U.S. foreign policy, leading to a more cautious and calculated approach in future military interventions. The Bay of Pigs invasion served as a lesson for future administrations, highlighting the need for thorough planning, intelligence accuracy, and decisive leadership.

Lastly, conspiracy theories and alternative explanations for Kennedy's decision further complicated the historical interpretations of the Bay of Pigs invasion. The lingering debates and speculation surrounding the true motives and intentions behind the watered-down invasion plan have had a lasting impact on how the event is understood and interpreted.

In conclusion, the impact on U.S.-Cuba relations moving forward was significant and multifaceted. From political and military consequences to intelligence failures and public perception, Kennedy's great mistake in watering down the Bay of Pigs invasion left a lasting imprint on U.S. foreign policy, Cold War dynamics, and historical interpretations.

Chapter 9: International Implications: Examining How Kennedy's Decision Affected US Relations with Other Countries, Particularly in Latin America and the Soviet Union

Latin American Reactions to the Bay of Pigs Invasion

The Bay of Pigs invasion in 1961 had far-reaching consequences, not only for the United States and Cuba but also for the rest of Latin America. This subchapter aims to examine the reactions of Latin American countries to this pivotal event in the Cold War era.

The invasion, carried out by a group of Cuban exiles with the support of the CIA, aimed to overthrow Fidel Castro's communist regime. However, the plan was poorly executed and ultimately failed, resulting in embarrassment for the United States and a strengthening of Castro's position.

Latin American countries had varying reactions to the Bay of Pigs invasion. Many governments, particularly those aligned with the

United States, expressed concern over the failure of the operation. They saw it as a setback in the fight against communism and feared that it would embolden leftist movements in their own countries. Some governments even condemned the United States for its involvement in the invasion, seeing it as an infringement on Cuban sovereignty.

On the other hand, left-leaning governments and anti-imperialist movements celebrated the failed invasion as a victory against American imperialism. They viewed the invasion as further evidence of U.S. interventionism and used it to rally support for their own anti-American agendas. This led to a surge in anti-American sentiment across Latin America and bolstered support for governments that opposed U.S. influence in the region.

The Bay of Pigs invasion also had a significant impact on U.S.-Latin American relations. The failure of the operation damaged the credibility of the United States and undermined its ability to rally support for its anti-communist agenda in the region. It also highlighted the United States' willingness to use covert operations to achieve its goals, which strained relations with many Latin American countries.

In conclusion, the Bay of Pigs invasion had a profound impact on Latin America. It not only affected the political landscape of the region but also shaped the perceptions of the United States among Latin American countries. The failed invasion further polarized the region, with some governments aligning themselves with the United States and others embracing anti-American sentiment. Understanding Latin American reactions to the Bay of Pigs invasion is crucial for historians analyzing the broader implications of this event in Cold War history.

The Impact on U.S. Influence in the Region

The subchapter titled "The Impact on U.S. Influence in the Region" delves into the consequences of President Kennedy's decision to water down the Bay of Pigs invasion plan for the United States' influence in the region. This chapter aims to provide historians with a comprehensive analysis of the long-lasting effects of Kennedy's actions on various aspects of U.S. foreign policy and international relations during the Cold War era.

One of the key areas that this subchapter explores is the political fallout resulting from Kennedy's decision. By analyzing the impact on Kennedy's reputation and the Democratic Party, historians can gain valuable insights into the consequences of the president's actions on public opinion and domestic politics. Additionally, the chapter examines how this decision affected Kennedy's leadership style and decision-making process, shedding light on the challenges he faced during this critical period in history.

Another important aspect addressed in this subchapter is the military implications of the diluted invasion plan. By evaluating the strategic consequences and the deviation from the original military objectives, historians can understand the operational failures and the impact on the outcome of the Bay of Pigs invasion. This analysis provides valuable insights into the military shortcomings and the lessons learned for future military operations.

Furthermore, the subchapter investigates the role of intelligence in shaping Kennedy's decision-making process. By exploring the intelligence failures and shortcomings that contributed to the decision to water down the invasion plan, historians can assess the impact of faulty intelligence on U.S. foreign policy and national security.

In addition to these aspects, the subchapter also explores the public opinion and media coverage of the event, analyzing how the media portrayed Kennedy's decision and the public's perception of it. Furthermore, it examines the impact on the Cuban exile community, their subsequent role in anti-Castro activities, and the long-term consequences for U.S.-Cuba relations.

This subchapter also compares Kennedy's approach to previous administrations, contrasting his handling of the Bay of Pigs invasion with the policies of previous presidents toward Cuba and the Soviet Union. By doing so, historians can gain a better understanding of the uniqueness of Kennedy's decision and its implications.

Lastly, the subchapter explores the international implications of Kennedy's decision, examining how it affected U.S. relations with other countries, particularly in Latin America and the Soviet Union. By analyzing these international reactions, historians can assess the impact of Kennedy's decision on the global stage.

In conclusion, the subchapter titled "The Impact on U.S. Influence in the Region" provides historians with a comprehensive analysis of the consequences of President Kennedy's decision to water down the Bay of Pigs invasion plan. By examining various aspects such as political fallout, military implications, leadership style, intelligence failures, public opinion, and international reactions, this subchapter offers valuable insights into the long-term consequences of Kennedy's actions and their impact on future U.S. foreign policy.

Soviet Union's Response to the Invasion

The Soviet Union's response to the Bay of Pigs invasion was a critical aspect of the overall historical narrative surrounding this ill-fated operation. As historians, it is essential to examine the Soviet Union's actions and reactions during this period to gain a comprehensive understanding of the events that unfolded.

At the time of the invasion, the Soviet Union was the United States' main adversary in the Cold War. Cuba, under the leadership of Fidel Castro, had aligned itself with the Soviet Union, making it a significant point of contention between the two superpowers. Understanding how the Soviets responded to the invasion provides valuable insights into the geopolitical dynamics of the era.

The Soviet Union closely monitored the situation in Cuba leading up to the Bay of Pigs invasion. They were aware of the United States' intentions and had been providing military and economic support to the Cuban government. When the invasion began on April 17, 1961, the Soviet leadership was quick to condemn the actions of the United States and lend their unequivocal support to Castro's regime.

Soviet Premier Nikita Khrushchev denounced the invasion as an act of aggression and imperialism. He saw it as a blatant violation of Cuban sovereignty and a direct threat to Soviet interests in the region. Khrushchev's response was forceful and unequivocal, warning the United States of dire consequences if they continued their interventionist activities in Cuba.

In the aftermath of the invasion, the Soviet Union ramped up its military presence in Cuba, providing additional arms, personnel, and economic aid. This move was seen as a direct response to the United States' actions and served to solidify the Soviet-Cuban alliance. The heightened tensions between the two superpowers in the aftermath of the invasion would eventually lead to the Cuban Missile Crisis in 1962, arguably the closest the world came to nuclear war during the Cold War.

The Soviet Union's response to the Bay of Pigs invasion had far-reaching implications. It strengthened the Soviet-Cuban alliance, deepened the divide between the United States and the Soviet Union, and heightened Cold War tensions. Understanding the Soviet Union's response is crucial to comprehending the overall impact of the invasion and its significance in the broader context of US-Soviet relations during the Cold War era.

The Impact on the Cold War Balance of Power

The Bay of Pigs invasion, a pivotal event in the history of the Cold War, had far-reaching consequences that significantly impacted the delicate balance of power between the United States and the Soviet Union. This subchapter aims to delve into the various dimensions of this impact, shedding light on the intricate dynamics of the era.

From a military standpoint, the diluted invasion plan had severe strategic implications. The original intention was to launch a full-scale assault, but President Kennedy's decision to water down the operation drastically reduced its effectiveness. As a result, the invading forces, comprised mostly of Cuban exiles, were ill-equipped and outnumbered. This miscalculation not only led to the invasion's failure but also exposed the vulnerabilities of the US military and its intelligence apparatus.

The political fallout of Kennedy's decision cannot be ignored either. The President's reputation suffered a major blow, as critics accused him of succumbing to Soviet pressure and compromising American interests. This decision also had long-lasting repercussions for the Democratic Party, which found itself under scrutiny for its handling of foreign policy issues during the Cold War era.

Kennedy's leadership style and decision-making process further exacerbated these consequences. By prioritizing caution and disregarding the advice of his military and intelligence advisors, Kennedy inadvertently revealed a lack of experience and strategic thinking. This not only undermined his credibility but also raised questions about his ability to handle future crises.

The role of intelligence failures in the decision-making process is also worth investigating. The subpar intelligence provided to Kennedy and his administration contributed to the flawed assessment of the invasion's prospects. This failure exposed the shortcomings of the intelligence community, necessitating a reevaluation of its methods and practices.

Public opinion and media coverage played a significant role in shaping the perception of Kennedy's decision. The media, with its extensive coverage of the invasion, influenced public sentiment and further damaged Kennedy's reputation. Moreover, the impact on the Cuban exile community cannot be understated. Their hopes for a successful invasion were shattered, leaving them disillusioned and fueling their subsequent involvement in anti-Castro activities.

In an attempt to contextualize Kennedy's decision, it is crucial to compare his approach to previous administrations' policies toward Cuba and the Soviets. Contrasting Kennedy's handling of the Bay of Pigs invasion with previous strategies highlights the unique challenges and complexities that he faced.

Internationally, Kennedy's decision had far-reaching implications. It strained US relations with not only the Soviet Union but also other Latin American countries, many of which viewed the invasion as a violation of sovereignty. This event also shaped future US foreign policy, particularly in terms of its approach to covert operations and interventionism.

The long-term consequences of Kennedy's decision cannot be ignored. It served as a painful lesson for the United States, forcing a reassessment of its Cold War strategies and foreign policy objectives. This event also fueled conspiracy theories and alternative interpretations, which continue to shape historical interpretations today.

In conclusion, the impact of Kennedy's decision to water down the Bay of Pigs invasion reverberated through various dimensions. From the military to the political, intelligence to public opinion, and international relations to long-term consequences, the ramifications of this event were profound and continue to shape our understanding of the Cold War era.

The Long-Term Diplomatic and Strategic Consequences

In the subchapter titled "The Long-Term Diplomatic and Strategic Consequences," we delve into the aftermath of President John F. Kennedy's decision to water down the Bay of Pigs invasion. This chapter explores the historical implications of Kennedy's actions and the far-reaching effects they had on various aspects of the Cold War era.

One of the key areas of analysis in this subchapter is the political fallout that ensued from Kennedy's decision. By examining the impact on Kennedy's reputation and the Democratic Party, historians gain a deeper understanding of how this event shaped the political landscape during the Cold War. It also provides insights into the challenges faced by Democratic leaders in maintaining a strong stance against communism while avoiding military escalation.

Furthermore, we explore the military implications of the diluted invasion plan. By evaluating the strategic consequences and the impact on military objectives and outcomes, historians gain valuable insights into the effectiveness of the operation and the potential missed opportunities. This analysis sheds light on the strengths and weaknesses of the US military and the challenges faced in executing complex covert operations.

The subchapter also delves into Kennedy's leadership style and decision-making process. By analyzing how these factors influenced the Bay of Pigs invasion, historians can better understand the motivations behind Kennedy's actions and the lessons learned from his leadership style. Additionally, we investigate the role of intelligence in this decision, exploring the failures and shortcomings that contributed to the watering down of the invasion plan.

Examining the public opinion and media coverage of the Bay of Pigs invasion provides another layer of understanding. By exploring how the media covered the event and the public's perception of Kennedy's decision, historians gain insights into the shaping of the narrative and its impact on public sentiment. This analysis helps to illuminate the complexities of managing public opinion during times of crisis.

We also analyze the impact on the Cuban exile community and their subsequent role in anti-Castro activities. By understanding the consequences of Kennedy's decision on this community, historians can better comprehend their motivations and contributions to subsequent events in US-Cuban relations.

Furthermore, the subchapter compares Kennedy's approach to previous administrations' policies toward Cuba and the Soviets. By contrasting his handling of the Bay of Pigs invasion with those of his predecessors, historians gain insights into the continuity or divergence of US foreign policy.

Finally, we explore the international implications of Kennedy's decision, particularly in Latin America and the Soviet Union. By examining how this decision affected US relations with other countries, historians can better understand the global ramifications of Kennedy's actions.

This subchapter also addresses the long-term consequences of Kennedy's decision and its impact on future US foreign policy. By assessing the lessons learned from this event, historians gain valuable insights into the formulation and execution of foreign policy strategies.

Lastly, we investigate conspiracy theories and alternative interpretations surrounding Kennedy's decision to water down the invasion plan. By exploring these theories and their impact on historical interpretations, historians gain a comprehensive understanding of the complexities surrounding this pivotal event in Cold War history.

Chapter 10: Lessons Learned: Assessing the Long-Term Consequences of Kennedy's Decision and Its Impact on Future US Foreign Policy

The Importance of Proper Planning and Strategic Objectives

In the realm of historical events, few have garnered as much attention and debate as the Bay of Pigs invasion. President John F. Kennedy's decision to water down the invasion plan has been the subject of intense scrutiny and analysis. This subchapter aims to delve into the significance of proper planning and strategic objectives in shaping the outcome of this ill-fated mission.

One of the key aspects that historians must examine is the political fallout of Kennedy's decision. By analyzing the impact on Kennedy's reputation and the Democratic Party during the Cold War era, we can gain valuable insights into the broader implications of this event. Did Kennedy's fear of the Soviets drive his decision to water down the invasion plan? How did this decision affect US foreign policy towards Cuba and the Soviets?

Furthermore, it is crucial to assess the military implications of the diluted invasion plan. By examining the strategic consequences and the impact on military objectives and outcomes, historians can gain a deeper understanding of the failures that occurred. Did the lack of proper planning and strategic objectives contribute to the mission's ultimate failure? How did this decision affect the morale and effectiveness of the military forces involved?

Equally important is evaluating Kennedy's leadership style and decision-making process. By analyzing his approach to the Bay of Pigs invasion, historians can shed light on his leadership strengths and weaknesses. Did Kennedy's decision-making process influence the outcome of the invasion? How did his leadership style impact the morale and effectiveness of the troops?

Another crucial aspect to explore is the role of intelligence failures and shortcomings. Investigating the intelligence failures that contributed to the decision to water down the invasion plan can provide valuable insights into the decision-making process. Were there missed opportunities or inaccurate assessments that influenced Kennedy's choice? How did these intelligence failures shape the subsequent actions of the administration?

The subchapter will also delve into the public opinion and media coverage surrounding the event. By exploring how the media covered the invasion and the public's perception of Kennedy's decision, historians can gain a comprehensive understanding of the impact on both domestic and international audiences.

Additionally, it is essential to analyze the impact on the Cuban exile community and their subsequent role in anti-Castro activities. How did Kennedy's decision affect the Cuban exile community's perception of the US government? Did it fuel or dampen their anti-Castro activities?

By comparing Kennedy's approach to previous administrations' policies towards Cuba and the Soviets, historians can uncover the nuances and differences in strategy. How did Kennedy's handling of the Bay of Pigs invasion differ from previous administrations? What were the implications of these differences?

Furthermore, exploring the international implications of Kennedy's decision is crucial. By examining how it affected US relations with other countries, particularly in Latin America and the Soviet Union, historians can assess the broader consequences of this event.

Lastly, this subchapter will assess the long-term consequences of Kennedy's decision and its impact on future US foreign policy. By evaluating the lessons learned from the Bay of Pigs invasion, historians can gain insights into the evolution of US foreign policy and the avoidance of similar mistakes in the future.

It is also imperative to investigate the conspiracy theories and alternative interpretations surrounding Kennedy's decision to water down the invasion plan. By delving into these theories and their impact on historical interpretations, historians can gain a more nuanced understanding of this pivotal moment in history.

In conclusion, proper planning and strategic objectives are of paramount importance in shaping the outcome of historical events such as the Bay of Pigs invasion. By examining the various aspects outlined in this subchapter, historians can unravel the truth behind Kennedy's great mistake and its far-reaching implications.

The Need for Accurate and Reliable Intelligence

In the realm of international affairs, the need for accurate and reliable intelligence cannot be overstated. This chapter delves into the crucial role that intelligence plays in decision-making, specifically in the context of the Bay of Pigs invasion. The failure to obtain and properly analyze intelligence had far-reaching implications that would ultimately contribute to President Kennedy's great mistake.

The Cuban Missile Crisis had heightened tensions between the United States and the Soviet Union, making it imperative for the Kennedy administration to have a clear understanding of the situation on the ground in Cuba. However, the intelligence community fell short in providing accurate and comprehensive information regarding the

Cuban military capabilities, the level of popular support for Fidel Castro's regime, and the potential reaction of the Soviet Union.

One of the biggest intelligence failures was the underestimation of the Cuban military's strength and the support it enjoyed from the Cuban people. This misjudgment led to a significant miscalculation in the planning of the invasion, resulting in an armed force that was ill-equipped and outnumbered. Had the intelligence accurately portrayed the reality of the situation, the decision to water down the invasion plan may have been reconsidered.

Furthermore, the intelligence community failed to properly assess the potential Soviet response to the invasion. The fear of direct confrontation with the Soviet Union was a driving factor behind the decision to reduce the scale and intensity of the operation. However, accurate intelligence regarding the Soviet Union's intentions and capabilities could have provided a more nuanced understanding of the risks involved.

The lack of accurate intelligence not only impacted the military outcomes of the invasion but also had broader political implications. The failure to accurately assess the level of popular support for Castro allowed the regime to portray the invasion as an act of aggression by the United States. This, in turn, had a detrimental effect on Kennedy's reputation and the Democratic Party's standing during the Cold War era.

In retrospect, the Bay of Pigs invasion serves as a stark reminder of the critical importance of accurate and reliable intelligence in foreign policy decision-making. The intelligence community must have the necessary resources, expertise, and support to gather and analyze information effectively. Without a solid foundation of intelligence, leaders are left to make decisions based on incomplete or flawed information, which can have grave consequences.

In the subsequent chapters, we will explore the impact of Kennedy's decision on various aspects, including the political fallout, military implications, leadership style, public opinion, and international relations. By examining these different angles, we hope to shed light on the multifaceted nature of this historical event and the lessons that can be learned from it.

The Influence of Political Considerations on Military Operations

In the subchapter titled "The Influence of Political Considerations on Military Operations" of the book "Kennedy's Great Mistake: Unveiling the Truth Behind the Watered-Down Bay of Pigs Invasion," we delve into the complex relationship between politics and military strategy. This subchapter addresses a niche audience of historians interested in various aspects of Kennedy's decision-making process and its wide-ranging implications.

Firstly, we analyze the political fallout of Kennedy's decision to water down the Bay of Pigs invasion for fear of the Soviets. We explore the impact on Kennedy's reputation and the Democratic Party during the Cold War era. By evaluating the strategic consequences of the diluted invasion plan, we examine the military implications and the resulting outcomes.

Furthermore, this subchapter delves into Kennedy's leadership style and decision-making process, analyzing how it influenced the Bay of Pigs invasion. We investigate the role of intelligence failures and shortcomings that contributed to the decision to water down the invasion plan. By exploring the media coverage and public perception of Kennedy's decision, we shed light on the power of public opinion and media in shaping historical events.

In addition, we assess the impact on the Cuban exile community and their subsequent role in anti-Castro activities. By contrasting

Kennedy's handling of the Bay of Pigs invasion with previous administrations' policies toward Cuba and the Soviets, we provide a comprehensive understanding of his approach.

Moreover, this subchapter examines the international implications of Kennedy's decision, particularly in Latin America and the Soviet Union. We analyze how this decision affected US relations with other countries and its long-term consequences on future US foreign policy.

Lastly, we investigate conspiracy theories and alternative explanations for Kennedy's decision to water down the invasion plan, and their impact on historical interpretations. By considering these alternate viewpoints, we encourage a critical analysis of the events surrounding the Bay of Pigs invasion.

Throughout this subchapter, we present a detailed examination of the influence of political considerations on military operations, focusing on Kennedy's decision to water down the Bay of Pigs invasion. By addressing the various niches within the audience of historians, we provide a comprehensive understanding of the events, their implications, and their place in history.

The Role of Public Opinion and Media Perception

"The Role of Public Opinion and Media Perception"

Public opinion and media perception played a significant role in shaping the aftermath of President John F. Kennedy's decision to water down the Bay of Pigs invasion. This subchapter seeks to analyze the impact of public opinion and media coverage on various aspects of this pivotal event in history.

One of the immediate effects of the diluted invasion plan was the political fallout on Kennedy's reputation and the Democratic Party during the Cold War era. Media coverage highlighted the perceived weakness of the President's decision, leading to a decline in public confidence and an erosion of support for the administration's foreign policy. Historians have since debated the extent to which this event influenced Kennedy's approach to subsequent foreign policy decisions.

Furthermore, the media's portrayal of the Bay of Pigs invasion had significant military implications. By downplaying the initial military objectives and outcomes, the public was left with a distorted perception of the operation. This led to a misjudgment of the strategic consequences of the diluted plan, impacting not only the military's ability to achieve its objectives but also the long-term implications for US foreign policy in the region.

Kennedy's leadership style and decision-making process also came under scrutiny through media coverage. Historians have examined how the President's reliance on a small circle of advisors and the pressure to avoid direct confrontation with the Soviets influenced his approach to the Bay of Pigs invasion. Understanding Kennedy's decision-making process sheds light on the factors that contributed to the watering down of the invasion plan.

The role of intelligence in the decision-making process cannot be overlooked. Media coverage and public opinion revealed intelligence failures and shortcomings that contributed to the decision to water down the invasion plan. These revelations further fueled public skepticism and raised questions about the reliability of US intelligence agencies.

The media coverage of the event and the public's perception of Kennedy's decision had a profound impact on the Cuban exile community. By highlighting the failure of the invasion and the subsequent abandonment of the exiles, the media inadvertently spurred anti-Castro sentiment and activism within the Cuban exile community.

Examining public opinion and media perception also requires a comparison of Kennedy's approach to previous administrations' policies toward Cuba and the Soviets. Contrasting his decisions with those of his predecessors provides insight into the unique challenges and political considerations that Kennedy faced during this critical period of the Cold War.

Furthermore, the international implications of Kennedy's decision need to be evaluated. The media coverage of the Bay of Pigs invasion affected US relations with other countries, particularly in Latin America and the Soviet Union. The perceived weakness of the US in this event shaped international perceptions and influenced future foreign policy decisions.

Lastly, this subchapter delves into conspiracy theories and alternative interpretations of Kennedy's decision. The media's coverage of the Bay of Pigs invasion fueled speculation and alternative explanations for the President's actions. Investigating these theories and their impact on historical interpretations allows historians to critically analyze the event and its broader implications.

In conclusion, the role of public opinion and media perception in the Bay of Pigs invasion cannot be underestimated. By exploring the impact on Kennedy's reputation, military outcomes, leadership style, intelligence failures, the Cuban exile community, international relations, and alternative interpretations, historians gain a comprehensive understanding of the significance of public opinion and media coverage in shaping historical narratives surrounding this critical event in American history.

Implications for Future US Foreign Policy and Military Interventions

The Bay of Pigs invasion, known as "Kennedy's Great Mistake," had far-reaching implications for future US foreign policy and military interventions. Historians have extensively analyzed the various aspects of this event, shedding light on its consequences and shaping our understanding of Cold War-era politics. This subchapter explores the multifaceted implications of Kennedy's decision to water down the invasion plan.

One significant implication was the political fallout of Kennedy's choice. By fearing Soviet retaliation, Kennedy compromised the mission's effectiveness and put his reputation and the Democratic Party at stake during a crucial period of the Cold War. Historians critically examine how this decision impacted Kennedy's standing domestically and internationally, as well as the subsequent implications for the Democratic Party's foreign policy approach.

Furthermore, the diluted invasion plan had significant military implications. By reducing the number of troops and air support, Kennedy compromised the operation's strategic objectives and outcomes. Historians analyze the military consequences, examining how the weakened invasion plan affected the mission's chances of success and its long-term impact on military interventions.

Kennedy's leadership style and decision-making process are also scrutinized. Historians delve into his approach, analyzing how his leadership style influenced the Bay of Pigs invasion. This examination sheds light on the factors that contributed to the watering down of the invasion plan, providing insights into Kennedy's decision-making and its implications.

The role of intelligence failures and shortcomings cannot be overlooked. Investigating these aspects is crucial to understanding why the decision to water down the invasion plan was made. Historians critically examine the intelligence community's failures and how they influenced the decision-making process, contributing to the overall outcome of the invasion.

Public opinion and media coverage played a significant role in shaping the perception of Kennedy's decision. Historians explore how the media covered the event and the public's reaction, providing insights into the impact of public opinion on Kennedy's reputation and the broader political landscape.

The Cuban exile community, which had high hopes for the invasion, experienced significant consequences as well. Historians analyze the impact of Kennedy's decision on the Cuban exile community and how it influenced their subsequent role in anti-Castro activities.

Comparisons with previous administrations' policies toward Cuba and the Soviets offer valuable insights into Kennedy's approach. By contrasting Kennedy's handling of the Bay of Pigs invasion with earlier administrations, historians provide a broader perspective on the long-standing issues surrounding US-Cuba relations.

Internationally, Kennedy's decision had implications for US relations with other countries, particularly in Latin America and the Soviet Union. Historians explore how this decision affected diplomatic relations, regional dynamics, and the overall global perception of US foreign policy.

Assessing the long-term consequences of Kennedy's decision is essential to understanding its impact on future US foreign policy. By analyzing the lessons learned from the Bay of Pigs invasion, historians can shed light on how this event influenced subsequent military interventions and shaped the trajectory of US foreign policy.

Finally, conspiracy theories and alternative interpretations abound regarding Kennedy's decision to water down the invasion plan. Historians investigate these theories and alternative explanations, analyzing their impact on historical interpretations and offering a comprehensive understanding of the event.

In conclusion, this subchapter delves into the implications of Kennedy's decision to water down the Bay of Pigs invasion. By exploring its impact on various aspects of US foreign policy, military interventions, and historical interpretations, historians can illuminate the far-reaching consequences of this pivotal event in Cold War history.

Chapter 11: Conspiracy Theories and Alternate Interpretations: Investigating Conspiracy Theories and Alternative Explanations for Kennedy's Decision to Water Down the Invasion Plan, and Their Impact on Historical Interpretations

The Conspiracy Theories Surrounding the Bay of Pigs

The Bay of Pigs invasion is one of the most infamous events in American history. It was a covert operation that aimed to overthrow the Cuban government led by Fidel Castro. However, the operation failed miserably, and its repercussions continue to reverberate to this day. While the failure of the invasion is well-documented, there are numerous conspiracy theories surrounding the events leading up to it.

One popular theory suggests that President John F. Kennedy intentionally watered down the invasion plan out of fear of provoking the Soviet Union. According to this theory, Kennedy was concerned that a full-scale invasion would escalate tensions between the United States and the Soviet Union, potentially leading to a nuclear war. As a result, he deliberately weakened the invasion force, leaving them ill-prepared and undermanned.

Another theory suggests that Kennedy was influenced by powerful individuals within his own administration who had their own agenda. These individuals, including members of the CIA and high-ranking officials, allegedly wanted to maintain the status quo in Cuba and prevent any drastic changes that could upset American interests in the region. They convinced Kennedy to reduce the size and strength of the invasion force, ensuring its failure.

Some conspiracy theories even go as far as to suggest that Kennedy had prior knowledge of the invasion's failure and allowed it to proceed anyway. These theories claim that Kennedy wanted to use the failed invasion as a pretext for further intervention in Cuba, with the ultimate goal of removing Castro from power. By allowing the invasion to fail, Kennedy could justify future military action without appearing reckless or aggressive.

These conspiracy theories have gained traction over the years, with historians and researchers delving into the details of the Bay of Pigs invasion to uncover the truth. While there is no concrete evidence to support these theories, they highlight the deep-rooted skepticism and mistrust that surrounded the events of that fateful day.

In conclusion, the conspiracy theories surrounding the Bay of Pigs invasion continue to captivate historians and researchers. While the official narrative suggests that the invasion failed due to a combination of factors, including poor planning and execution, these theories offer alternate explanations for the events that transpired. Whether they hold any truth or not, they shed light on the complexities and uncertainties surrounding one of the darkest chapters in American history.

11

Subchapter 11: Conspiracy Theories and Alternate Interpretations

In the realm of historical events, there is often a plethora of conspiracy theories and alternative interpretations that emerge over time. The Bay of Pigs invasion is certainly no exception. In this subchapter, we delve into the various conspiracy theories surrounding Kennedy's decision to water down the invasion plan and explore alternative explanations that challenge the traditional narrative.

One prevalent conspiracy theory suggests that Kennedy intentionally weakened the invasion plan to appease the Soviets and prevent a potential nuclear war. Proponents argue that Kennedy, fearing the escalation of tensions with the Soviet Union, deliberately sabotaged the operation to avoid a catastrophic conflict. This theory is fueled by the fact that Kennedy's decision to reduce the air support and cancel the second wave of airstrikes seemed to benefit the Soviets and Castro's regime.

Another alternative interpretation posits that Kennedy was influenced by political considerations, specifically the upcoming 1962 midterm elections. Critics argue that Kennedy, facing a difficult political climate, may have chosen to prioritize his own party's political fortunes over the success of the invasion. By downplaying the operation and minimizing its potential impact, he may have hoped to avoid a public backlash in the event of failure.

Furthermore, some historians argue that Kennedy's leadership style and decision-making process played a significant role in the watered-down invasion plan. They contend that Kennedy's tendency to rely heavily on a small circle of advisors, known as the "best and the brightest," contributed to a lack of diverse perspectives and critical analysis. This may have resulted in a flawed decision-making process that ultimately weakened the invasion plan.

While conspiracy theories and alternative interpretations can provide valuable insights and challenge conventional wisdom, it is important to approach them with caution. The historical evidence supporting these theories often lacks substantial backing or is based on speculative assumptions. Nevertheless, their existence underscores the enduring controversy and intrigue surrounding the Bay of Pigs invasion.

As historians, it is our duty to critically analyze and evaluate these theories, drawing upon primary sources, testimonies, and objective analysis. By doing so, we can gain a deeper understanding of the complex factors that influenced Kennedy's decision and its long-term consequences. Ultimately, our goal is to unravel the truth behind the watered-down Bay of Pigs invasion and shed light on the multitude of perspectives that shape our understanding of this pivotal event in Cold War history.

www.ingramcontent.com/pod-product-compliance
Lightning Source LLC
Chambersburg PA
CBHW031124160726
47989CB00016B/1004